JOURNEY TO DRAWING AND PAINTING

College Admissions & Profiles

Rachel A. Winston, Ph.D.

Lizard Publishing is not sponsored by any college. While data was derived by school, state, or nationally published sources, some statistics may be out of date as published sources vary widely based upon the date of submission and currency of numbers. Attempts were made to obtain the best information during the writing of this book from, NCES, U.S. Census Bureau, U.S. Department of Education, Common Data Set, College Board, U.S. News & World Report, college, and organizational sites. Descriptions of colleges are a compilation of college website information as well as student, faculty, and staff interviews with individuals and often from unique experiences and impressions. Attempts were made to triangulate multiple points of light. If you would like to share program information, data, or an impression of a specific college, please write to Lizard Publishing at the address below or at the e-mail address: *collegeguide@yahoo.com*

ISBN 978-1946432766 (hardback); 978-1946432759 (paperback); 978-1946432773 (e-book)

LCCN: 2022908434

Lizard Publishing, 7700 Irvine Center Drive, Suite 800, Irvine, CA 92618 *www.lizard-publishing.com*

Lizard Publishing creates, designs, produces, and distributes books and resources to provide academic, admissions, and career information. Our mental process is fueled by three tenets:

- Ignite the hunger to learn and the passion to make a difference
- Illuminate the expanse of knowledge by sharing cutting edge thinking
- Innovate to create a world that makes the transition from dreams to reality

We work with academic leaders who transform the educational landscape to publish relevant content and advise students of their educational and professional options, with the aim of developing 21st-century learners and leaders. We also work with students to publish their books and present widely diverse ideas to the college/graduate school-bound community. With headquarters in Irvine, California, Lizard Publishing works virtually with authors to edit, publish, and distribute both hard copy and paperback books.

This book was published in the U.S.A. Lizard Publishing is a premium quality provider of educational reference, career guidance, and motivational publications/merchandise for global learners, educators, and stakeholders in education.

Book design by Michelle Tahan *www.michelletahan.com*

Book formatting by Obinna Chinemerem Ozuo

Book website: *www.collegelizard.com*

LIZARD PUBLISHING

This book is dedicated to Katie Foose and Cecilia Yang, who epitomize dedication, multi-dimensional talent, and professionalism.

ACKNOWLEDGMENTS

There is never enough room to acknowledge every person. Numerous people contributed to my perspective about art. Students, faculty, counselors, and researchers assisted in enhancing my knowledge base or taught me indelible lessons. Over a lifetime of experiences working with students, I am wiser and more worldly.

I gratefully acknowledge Michelle Tahan, Jasmine Jhunjhnuwala, E. Liz Kim, and Jacqueline Xu, as well as my family, friends, colleagues, and professors. With profound gratitude, I also acknowledge those I have known in the art world.

As a faculty member in the UCLA College Counseling Certificate Program, I met many dedicated counselors who spend their life serving and supporting students. Meaningful contributions to the book have been made indirectly by admissions representatives, college counselors, and faculty members who took a special interest in this book's success.

I would also like to thank the thousands of students I have taught, counseled, or supported in my nearly four decades of service.

"If I see so far, it is because I stand on the shoulders of giants."
– Isaac Newton

Isaac Newton once said, "If I see so far, it is because I stand on the shoulders of giants." A few of those giants whose broad shoulders lifted me higher and helped teach invaluable lessons include Kendall May, Bowie Deng, Emma Farkas, Sarah Huang, William Wolf, Shylee Roohian, Keyon Sabahi, Monette Tarvaran, Junheng Xu, Emily Liu, Daniel Wolf, Dania Olia, Anya Behrms, and Stefy Lin.

Finally, there would be no book on drawing and painting programs and no career in college admissions counseling without the support of Robert Helmer, whose tireless efforts support me every single day.

ABOUT THE AUTHOR

D r. Rachel A. Winston is a tireless student advocate. She has served the educational community as a university professor, college advisor, statistician, researcher, author, cryptanalyst, motivational speaker, publishing executive, and lifelong student. As one of the leading experts in college counseling and an award-winning faculty member, Dr. Winston has spent her lifetime learning, teaching, mentoring, and coaching students. Her counseling practice centers around college admissions, college essays, portfolios, and intellectual conversations about life and career pursuits.

She started college at thirteen and graduated from college programs in such widely ranging disciplines as chemistry, mathematics, computers, liberal arts, international relations, negotiation, conflict resolution, peacebuilding, business administration, higher education leadership, interpreting, college counseling, and publishing. Throughout her education, she attended and graduated from Harvard, University of Chicago, University of Texas, GWU, UCLA, Syracuse, CSUF, CSUDH, Pepperdine, Claremont Graduate University, and Gallaudet University.

Her position working in Washington, D.C. on Capitol Hill and with the White House in the 1980s took her to approximately a hundred universities training campaign managers at colleges from Colorado to California, thoroughly dotting the western states. Later, she led college tours with students and their families on road trips throughout the United States. She has taught or counseled thousands of students over her career and speaks at conferences and academic programs throughout the world.

As a professor and avid writer for numerous publications, she won the 2012 McFarland Literary Achievement Award, Bletchley Park Cryptanalyst Award, and numerous other awards, including Faculty Member of the Year, Leadership Tomorrow Leader of the Year, and college service and leadership awards. While studying Human Capital at Claremont Graduate University, she was a scholarship recipient at the Drucker School of Management. She was also elected to the statewide Board of Governors for the Faculty Association for California Community Colleges, where she served on the executive committee.

She also served as a faculty member for the UCLA College Counselor Certificate Program, the Director of Mathematics at Brandman University, and Embry Riddle Aeronautical University, Chapman University, Cal State Fullerton, and a handful of California Community Colleges, including Cerro Coso College where she represented the entire faculty as the Academic Senate President and retired in 2016. Over her career, she taught mathematics online, on television, live interactive satellite, telecourses, and in large and small lecture halls.

AUTHOR'S NOTE

You are reading this book because you are considering admission to colleges where you open the doors to the world of art, design, and creativity. Whatever route you took to get to this point, you are in the right place. Right now, you need to gather information to make informed decisions.

While many people offer advice, suggestions differ. Friends will tell you the 'right' way or the way their neighbor was accepted. Graciously accept this anecdotal information, pursuing imaginative artistry with your heart and mind as you commit to learning more.

Dig deeper to consider both expert and current information from counselors who have worked with hundreds of students. Changes in programs, curricula, requirements, and links happen each year.

Doublecheck each program's specifics yourself. Each school's profile information is current as of April 2022. However, since researching this book, changes may have taken place. There are other college guidebooks written by talented and experienced counselors, though none like this book on college programs for drawing and painting. Nevertheless, I admire and cheer on their efforts.

"We are what we think. All that we are arises with our thoughts. With our thoughts, we make the world."
— Buddha

This book, providing lists of colleges, admissions information, and profiles, is different in that it also offers unique tidbits. I hope you find the information valuable. Your job is to begin early by assembling lists of possible schools to consider. Create a road map and set yourself on a clear path.

If you see an error in this book or even a suggestion for a future edition, please write to Dr. Rachel A. Winston at collegeguide@yahoo.com. We will fix the entry with the next printed version. All of that said, this book was written with you in mind.

This book contains a wealth of information on the Internet with free downloads, FAQs, testimonials, and offers to help you with your applications. Some advisors are knowledgeable and provide valuable assistance. Unfortunately, students and parents hunt around the web, searching for a tremendous number of hours to seek the information they need. This book aims to resolve this problem with college admissions data and profiles to make your search easier.

For now, though, I will assume you want to attend college to study art and are exploring this book to find a program that will get you on your way toward your goal. You are undoubtedly a talented candidate who is willing to work very hard. Creative mental exploration is virtually a prerequisite for art programs.

As you investigate colleges, you might find that some programs are listed in different college departments. Either way, this book will help you reach your goal. Applying to and writing essays for each application will require research to determine which program is right for you and the specific reasons you are a good fit.

While you might believe that art-focused colleges are relatively similar, each program's nuances make them very different. These small differences may seem confusing. My goal with this book is to demystify the information and process.

CONTENTS

CHAPTER 1

CAPTURING PEOPLE'S IMAGINATION: TURNING IDEAS INTO ART

"Creativity takes courage."

– Henri Matisse

Artists make work that inspires and buoys us in difficult times, reminding us of the valuable things in life.

- Romain Rolland

WONDER, INQUISITIVENESS, AND IMAGINATION

With the stroke of a brush, paint is applied to a canvas. The first application begins the conversion from blankness into art. From then on, the artist's imagination flows from idea to imagery. Captivating and thought-provoking, a painter's artistry transforms a page into that which has never before been seen in exactly the same way. Sketches and paintings reveal stories that are not otherwise told. Ideas come to fruition. Over the course of time, a composition made with pencils, charcoal, pastels, and brushes comes alive. The artist breathes life into inspiration.

Art's role in society is immensely important and often underappreciated. Artists capture thoughts, like chasing butterflies that flap their wings over a grassy lawn. Moments come alive as a painting emerges from that blissful day. Ideas skip in the mind, dancing with Georgia O'Keefe's abstract flowers in childlike wonder. Pablo Picasso once said, "Every child is an artist, the problem is staying an artist when you grow up."

Paintings present ideas in various forms for a variety of audiences. While most people think about fine art in museums, galleries, businesses, and homes, art's usefulness is widespread. Art adds meaning to life and allows audiences to interpret works in whatever ways speak to them. While what we see does influence what we create, new creations are not mere mimicry no matter how natural the impulse to imitate. Furthermore, audiences react differently as well.

ORIGINS OF ART

The prehistoric origins of art lie within Africa. Art served as a tool to communicate and preserve ideas and innovations. With an aesthetic appeal, creatively designed symbols and patterns defined humans' unique characteristics. Ideas and ways of life passed from generation to generation. Scientists believe the Neanderthal made the petroglyphs, the first art known to exist, approximately 65,000 years ago. Patterns with color, skin colorings with ochre, and beads for decoration were likely the first forms of art, though little information is available.

Homo sapiens migrated from Africa approximately 45,000 years ago as determined by artifacts found in Europe. Migrations continued to Asia too. New findings, though, show that the oldest cave painting, 45,500 years old, was found in Indonesia and etchings found in Germany are thought to be 51,000 years old.[1] Thousands of years later, 2-D and 3-D art emerged with curves, lines, products, tools, and manmade bowls. Examples of art appeared in other forms too, including European cave paintings and decorations. Written records were also found, providing documented evidence of early forms of music, dance, storytelling, and poetry.

With such a long history and trillions of examples produced over the millennia, humans' fascination for art offer insights into the evolution of creative inspirations. Today, art takes on a widening array of possibilities.

USING NEW TECHNOLOGIES TO AWE AND INSPIRE

This moment is exciting. New paradigms of drawing and painting awaken as technology expands, disrupting every facet of life. Thus, we live in a time when rapid change will require that we think differently and consider art from a new pair of glasses. The future of humanity and all other living things depends on those who can think past today, imagine tomorrow, and solve problems along the way. You live at a critical juncture where 5G, 6G, and 7G will mesh with digital currencies and Metaverse spaces. We will barely recognize our current existence by 2050. Much of that transformation will happen as a function of innovators who will invent tomorrow.

---

1   Amy McDermott, 2021. "What was the first 'art'? How would we know?" *PNAS*, October 27, 2021. https://www.pnas.org/doi/10.1073/pnas.2117561118

Using oils, acrylics, watercolors, gouache, and new types of paint, flowers, landscapes, people, and wildlife emerge from a canvas. The most popular style is realism, which reconstructs an object or scene with light, shading, and tone. Photorealism looks as realistic as a photograph. Painterly does not hide textures and movement in its use of brushstrokes, while impressionism appears unfinished with its visibly small, disconnected brushstrokes. Abstract paintings use shapes, colors, and textures to leave the painting's meaning to the observer. Finally, surrealism offers seemingly local images expressed in an imaginative or illogical way. Every style offers unique possibilities to the painter and observer alike.

CHALLENGING CONVENTION

The definition of unique is to be different. Uninhibited creativity is fundamental to art, while inquisitive experimentation is integral to blazing a trail toward your distinctive style. However, not everything you try will work. Some ideas will suffer the slings and arrows of those around you who question your abilities or simply cannot understand your creations. You can continue unabated or try something new. Feedback is good, though it sometimes stings. Use the feedback or not.

This is your journey, not theirs. After all, this is art. It is your imagination you are letting loose. In this space of vulnerability, you may feel insecure. Keep pushing through to new possibilities. Remember that, while Vincent van Gogh may be one of the greatest painters of all time, the Dutch post-impressionist suffered enormous hardships in his personal and professional life. Sadly, he achieved worldwide fame and success after his lifetime.

Success is sometimes the outcome of a whole string of failures.

– Vincent van Gogh

Magdalena Carmen Frida Kahlo y Calderó, better known as Frida Kahlo, sought and found her unique path by painting self-portraits. Though she became extremely successful, her life also took unfortunate turns which led her down meandering roadways.

Disabled with polio as a child, she was later seriously injured in a bus accident. Her intellectual pursuits gave way to her artistic interests. Unwilling to let her physical limitations prevent her from exploring her imagination, she allowed her creative juices to flow freely. Kahlo constructed brilliantly colorful settings with characters adorned in ornate costumes as she explored the themes of self-identity, psychological power, and rebellious inspiration. Inspiring future generations while infusing Mexican culture and European fashion, she once said,

Feet, what do I need you for when I have wings to fly?

– Frida Kahlo

HOPE AND PRAGMATISM

As an experimentalist, you will construct the foundation for civilization's future. Begin this journey by stepping into the possibilities of today and the augmented realities of tomorrow. There are many directions you can take with your creative artistry. The combination of complex concepts will add to the challenge and intrigue of your career. The programs and colleges profiled in this book offer varied paths for you to explore. Choose the direction that makes the most sense to you. The information contained within will lead you on your way.

I dream of painting and then I paint my dream.

– Vincent Van Gogh

CHAPTER 2

THE MANY FORMS OF ART MAKING: THE WORLD OF ART BECKONS YOU TO ENTER

"If I could say it in words there would be no reason to paint."

— **Edward Hopper**

n studio spaces, creativity is unleashed. Artists, inspired to invent the future, blend vision and wonder with the nuts and bolts of the tools of their trade. Students studying drawing and painting are invited to set free the barriers of their minds-eye and visualize what has yet to be considered. Space and time, limiting to some, is merely a given entity in which to create. The possible career pursuits are only limited by your imagination.

SELLING YOUR ART

Unsurprisingly, more people are purchasing art online than in any other location. The pandemic closed many galleries. Some moved their artwork online and are seeing more sales via the Internet than in their showroom. However, there are also a wide array of online stores offering avenues to sell your art. This moment is exciting since there is a range of possibilities for your work to be shown and for you to be paid for your creative genius. Art of all kinds can be sold in these virtual shops from drawings, paintings, and illustrations to ceramics, sculptures, and crafts.

With fewer middlemen taking a cut, an artist can fluidly transition directly from canvas to screen to customer. For example, FineArtAmerica offers independent artists a venue to sell their wall art as framed or canvas prints, posters or art prints, or in collections of apparel, tapestries, or tech-centered. They boast of selling more than five million museum-quality products to buyers worldwide. It's fun just flipping through the screens of paintings, photographs, digital art, illustrations, mixed media, and originals. There is even a "Meet the Artist" center where you can post your story and your art.

ArtPal also represents more than two hundred thousand artists. Since ArtPal is a free gallery with no membership fees, buyers can browse and shop without the hassle of some of the other sites. Artists can sell their items or set the site for print on demand. Custom framing is another feature buyers appreciate. ArtPal sells art in the following categories - paintings & prints, photography, drawings & illustrations, digital art, sculptures & carvings, ceramics & pottery, glass, jewelry, textile & apparel, crafts, and other art. Browse the site just to get inspiration. Merely reading some of the bios could be inspirational. A few are in multiple languages.

Well, Amazon sells pretty much everything, but Amazon Art is a viable venue for 2-D art. Unfortunately, 3-D art is not included, but there is a location to sell crafts at Amazon Handmade. In the Amazon Art area, you can click on acrylic, oil, archival digital, watercolor, lithographs, landscape, floral, animals, architecture, nautical, and maps. You can also shop by height, width, color, or price. Since there are so many choices, use the search tool on the left side to help you sort through the thousands of offerings. Merely flipping through the digital pages will inspire you to stop what you are doing and get back to creating your art.

For those passionate about art, there are numerous other third-party websites like ArtFinder, ArtNet, ArtPlease, ArtPlode, Art Storefronts, Artsy, Azucar Gallery, Casetify, Displate, Ebay, Etsy, Minted, OnlineGallery.art, Picta Design, RedBubble, Saatchi Art, Shopify, Singulart, Society6, Storenvy, UGallery, Vsual, and Zazzle. While I do not recommend any specific site over another, these are good places to consider selling your art. Of course, you have greater control by selling your work on your own website, but you need a fanbase first that you can build through friend groups, teaching, lectures, or social media. Additionally, you can also make art to order on Fiverr.

Most people enjoy expressions of art in their homes and offices. Art inspires, reflecting our deeper thoughts and the world around us. Creating, sharing, and displaying art are fun ways to live life expressively. As you plan your future, remember, there are many possible doors to enter. You just need to choose the right one for you.

FOR LOVE OR MONEY
PURSUE ART FOR YOUR DESIRE TO CREATE

If you hunger to explore art, you are in the right place. Motivational author, Marsha Sinetar, said, "Do what you love, and the money will follow." Thus, if art is your passion, you will either make your living as a professional artist, pursue art as a hobby, or translate the lessons you learn to another career or field of interest. You will learn how to use various media, for sure. However, in college, you will also learn storytelling through words and art, social media marketing, communication, presentation, and inventiveness. Each morning you will awaken with a burning desire to create or simply experiment.

The knowledge you obtain in college might also take you on a path towards education. Teaching is a noble field, offering endless inspiration. Kids, eager to experiment, use art as a form of play, diving into their paint and canvas with unbridled exuberance. Mahatma Gandhi once said, "If you want real peace in the world, start with children." Their innocence, enthusiasm, and idealism remove the bounds of learned anger and resentment. You can touch the future by empowering kids through the medium of art. You will be surprised at what they can produce when they are led on a path toward peace, possibility, and friendship.

Though you might consider teaching in a local school or college, private classes offer another option. No matter what you do with your skills, you will have opportunities to use them for the rest of your life.

MUCH TO LEARN IN COLLEGE

Studying art in college will not only teach you new techniques, but allow you to examine, test, and collaborate with those who have similar interests. You will pursue a curriculum of classes in an inspirational community, leading you to advance your skills and inspiring you to push the bounds of your creativity. Professional artists who serve as your professors have impressive credentials and share their wisdom. You will learn in a unique studio environment surrounded by other extraordinarily talented individuals.

Ultimately, your portfolio will be your calling card, not your classes, professors, or colleges you choose to attend. There is no shortcut to success in this field, though learning to market yourself is essential. Diligence is required as you differentiate yourself as an artist with a distinctive style. Networking is also invaluable, supported by a talent pool of amazing students and professors who have connections. You do not need a college education to be successful, though it can open doors.

You will learn how to manage time and quickly evaluate your creations while evaluating the status of your projects. You will also gain valuable feedback from your peers. On group projects, collaborating can be challenging and exhilarating at the same time. Each member must listen attentively and conceptualize options while proposing ideas and creating a clear line of communication. By discussing opportunities for improvement, students can efficiently and effectively cooperate in crafting the best outcome.

The journey you are taking will have its ups and downs, but you will have stories to tell for the rest of your life. Your education may have unpredictable elements, and pitfalls may lay in your path. Since you have endured a pandemic and the repercussions of a war, you are imbued with a few doses of resilience. You will be tested in your arts-focused program as there is much to learn in a short amount of time.

You are embarking on a thrilling, demanding, and disciplined pursuit. You will work with extremely skilled and brilliant students who started creating art and crafts when they entered elementary school. Some have worked in businesses and have talents that will blow you away. Some classmates will produce professional-quality artwork. Do not let their abilities bring you down or make you feel as if you are not good enough. On the contrary, you will add your element and learn more during college. Besides, your enthusiasm will show through in your work and effort. Recognizing your potential, commitment, and attitude, people will be awed at your creations as you also step back to appreciate your work.

Enjoy the experience.

CHAPTER 3

ACADEMIC PREPARATION: ART, LIFE, AND SCHOOL FOUNDATIONS FOR FUTURE COURSEWORK

"I found I could say things with color and shapes that I couldn't say any other way — things I had no words for."

– Georgia O'Keeffe

Y ou are headed toward art mastery. To gain admission to your dream college you must be smart and talented. Even if the admission's requirements do not require a portfolio, and many do, to be successful, there are numerous preparatory skills you must develop as if you were presenting your work to a committee. Plan for your future now. Talent is only the beginning.

In high school, or college if you plan to transfer into a program, you must build solid skills in studio training inside and/or outside of school. The more exceptional artwork you can present to an admissions committee within their guidelines the better. Some mix of drawing, painting, ceramics, sculpture, 3-D design, and digital art are key components of a portfolio, though not all of these skills are necessary. Some applicants have never taken graphic design or sculpture and are not penalized. Nevertheless, foundational skills in your craft and art theory are important.

COMPELLING REASONS TO STUDY DRAWING & PAINTING

1. Freedom of creative expression
2. Mind explosion of ideas and possibilities
3. Love for experimentation with colors, forms, styles, shapes, and media
4. Sensory experience when witnessing captivating imagery
5. Emotional feeling that beckons you into art's space
6. The chance to turn your love into a lifetime career
7. Self-expression, self-confidence, and self-awareness
8. Individuality, unique flair, and distinctive style

IS ATTENDING COLLEGE FOR DRAWING & PAINTING WORTH IT?

Art has the power to relieve stress and awaken the senses. School is often unempowering for those who are disenchanted with memorizing chapters of text, reading endless charters, and solving problems that seem to have no practical use. Learning math, science, and history present a one-size-fits-all model, where everyone marches in line and dutifully follows the requirements. However, there is something useful, presentable, and magical about art.

In its many forms, art enlivens. If you have practiced art, you may have a favorite medium to express yourself and define your distinct style. However, with a degree concentrated on drawing and painting, you will learn many additional styles and techniques.

The immersive college experience will expose you to the practices of great artists and alternative methodologies of contemporary idea generators today. You will discover a wide range of options in each art class and determine the styles and techniques you prefer. Instructors, guest lecturers, and workshop hosts will help you continue to improve your skills while offering you feedback to go to the next level.

CAN ARTISTS MAKE A LIVING?

Since money and time are valuable commodities, the question of worth, value, and future income always crop up in my college counseling sessions. Consider your future wisely before making such a big decision, though I believe that "where there is a will, there is a way." This means, of course, that you must be dedicated to your craft, have a vision for where you are headed, be persistent in taking opportunities to practice, and have the wisdom to make smart choices.

In a world where social media can connect you to customers, you can display your art through many different sites without leaving your studio, which may be your apartment. You may choose to be an intrepid frontrunner by creating a gallery in the Metaverse and selling your artwork using NFTs, bitcoin, or another digital payment system.

Amazing college professors who are successful in their own right will suggest ways to sell your art and may even link you to their contacts. In the process, you will discover your brand of professionalism along with a calling card of images that allow others to understand what you offer.

"THERE IS NO ROYAL ROAD TO GEOMETRY" - EUCLID

When a student asked Euclid if there was an easier way to learn geometry, he cautioned that discipline and persistence are essential. Hard work is absolutely necessary. Additionally, there is no one way to succeed, just as there is no one way to paint. You may choose to draw images for a company, sell your paintings, teach others fine arts, or support other artists by sharing your wisdom. Either way, art is a versatile skill. Other professional options include arts management, museum studies, television, entertainment, fashion, education, art therapy, and much more.

You could manage an art store or create your own online webstore. You might find that critiquing art is of interest or helping other people market their art is empowering. Museums have a variety of positions that require the knowledge of trained artists.

Teaching is often considered a fallback. Yet, many people who choose to teach are inspired by the innocence and dreams of young artists. Finally, art therapy has excellent potential to make a difference in someone's life. So many people were demoralized by the pandemic and could not find their way forward toward hope and possibility. You could support others to find their peace of mind. My point is that, as you develop your skills, your talent is not wasted, not lost, not valueless. You can be a source of empowerment and strength for others.

ARTS MANAGEMENT

This field has grown in the past decade as more people seek ways to contemplate life through art. The job of an arts manager is to know and understand art while also having a business sense to manage a private or public art institution. Thus, arts managers efficiently run the business and share the creative inspirations of artists, performers, or designers. With skills in planning events, managing talent, envisioning space, communicating messages, and hosting guests, you will serve society in significant ways. For example, suppose you want to inspire both artists and patrons alike, giving artists the freedom to express themselves while offering visitors or purchasers the chance to learn, identify, feel, and imagine. In that case, arts management is an excellent profession, and it can pay well.

ARTS/ENTERTAINMENT AGENT

This profession is perfect for the person who is inspired to help artists find locations to promote, show, and sell their artwork. Many times, artists consume themselves in their art. They immerse themselves in the vision and technical precision of their craft. However, they are not skilled in public relations, advertising, promotion, website development, social media, and the legal aspects of contracts, releases, and intellectual property. Many artists want to focus on their art rather than pounding the pavement to find shows, exhibitions, events, venues, and other opportunities. Here, an agent may be invaluable.

An arts/entertainment agent ensures that excellent art of all kinds has a platform to be seen. Imagine for a moment how many thousands of extraordinarily talented artists exist whose work is never seen except possibly among a small enclave of other talented artists or friends. Thus, those who are 'successful' are 'discovered' or promoted. They are not always the best artists. You might find representing talented people uplifting. Otherwise, you might contract with an arts/entertainment agent yourself.

FASHION DESIGN, TEXTILE DESIGN, AND MERCHANDISING

Painters with an eye for color, style, and design often express this through their own hair, clothing, or accessories. Often, they enjoy pondering other individuals' attires as models of fashion or ways to augment their look. Starting with envisioning and sketching fabric designs before they are woven, or designing them after the cloth is created, there is an immense amount of artistry involved with clothing creation. Attending fashion shows, buying next season's designs, marketing outfits, and displaying items in stores takes the flair of a creative mind. Individuals with these interests may discover that segments of the fashion industry are immensely appealing.

TEACHING, EDUCATION, AND TRAINING

Kids clamor to create. Their imaginations run wild with ideas. Self-expression and exploration through art offer people young and old the chance to put their ideas onto paper, a computer, or a still/moving medium like photography or film. Some perform in voice, dance, and acting. As a result, there are numerous jobs in private and public education. Schools everywhere hire art teachers. Families hire art coaches. Private studios conduct workshops and training. College art professors can make $100,000/year teaching students while continuing to practice their craft.

In the United States, in 2021, there were approximately 130,000 public and private K-12 schools, according to the National Center for Educational Statistics. Furthermore, during the 2019-2020 school year, there were 3,982 degree-granting higher education colleges and universities – 2,679 4-year and 1,303 2-year institutions.[1] In California alone, during the 2020-2021 school year, there were 10,545 K-12 public schools and another 1,296 charter schools.[2] Thus, there are numerous schools in which you may choose to work.

1   NCES, "Digest of Education Statistics," U.S. Department of Education, 2020 Tables and Figures, https://nces.ed.gov/programs/digest/d20/tables/dt20_317.10.asp

2   California Department of Education, "Fingertip Facts on Education in California", 2020-2021, https://www.cde.ca.gov/ds/ad/ceffingertipfacts.asp

ART THERAPY

Art therapists are clinicians who support people of all ages as mental health practitioners. They provide services and counseling through the active practice of art-making and other creative processes. Art can be a healing power, allowing individuals to improve their physical and mental abilities while reducing both stress and conflict and improving both self-esteem and self-awareness. Using applied psychology, art therapists improve the human experience in a psychotherapeutic relationship. Art therapists must be credentialed and certified to practice in hospitals, schools, veteran's clinics, private practice, rehabilitation centers, psychiatric facilities, community clinics, crisis centers, forensic institutions, and senior communities.

To become an art therapist, you must attend graduate school and earn a master's or doctoral degree. However, there are undergraduate programs in art therapy that can get you on your way. A Master of Arts in Art Therapy can also lead to a Master of Arts in Marriage and Family Studies or a Ph.D. in Art Therapy. Most graduate programs prepare graduates to sit for the Art Therapy Registration (ATR), Licensed Creative Arts Therapist (LCAT), and Licensed Professional Clinical Counselor (LPCC).

UNDERGRADUATE ART THERAPY PROGRAMS
AMERICAN ART THERAPY ASSOCIATION

Anna Maria College (MA)

Capital University (OH)

Converse College (SC)

Edgewood College (WI)

Long Island University, Post Campus (NY)

Mars Hill University (NC)

Mercyhurst University (PA)

Millikin University (IL)

Mount Mary University (WI)

Notre Dame of Maryland Univ. (MD)

Russell Sage College (NY)

Seton Hill University (PA)

St. Thomas Aquinas College (NY)

Temple University (PA)

University of the Arts (PA)

University of Tampa (FL)

Ursuline College (OH)

CAAHEP ACCREDITED GRADUATE ART THERAPY PROGRAMS[3]

Adler Graduate School (MN)

Albertus Magnus College (CT)

Antioch University Seattle (WA)

Caldwell University (NJ)

Drexel University (PA)

Eastern Virginia Medical School (VA)

Edinboro University (PA)

Emporia State University (KS)

Florida State University (FL)

George Washington University (DC)

Hofstra University (NY)

Indiana Univ.-Purdue Univ.-IUPUI (IN)

Lewis & Clark College (OR)

Long Island University – Post (NY)

Loyola Marymount University (CA)

Maywood University (PA)

Naropa University (CO)

Nazareth College (NY)

New York University (NY)

Southern Illinois University (IL)

Southwestern College (NM)

Springfield College (MA)

St. Mary-of-the-Woods College (IN)

University of Louisville (KY)

Ursuline College (OH)

3   CAAHEP, "Commission on Accreditation" https://www.caahep.org/Students/Find-a-Program.aspx

LIMITLESS POSSIBILITIES

The preparation you receive as an art student will not restrict you. One of my students went from painting to game design, which required a year of focused digital skills, but he now has an amazing job that he enjoys. Drawing and painting are fundamental to any area of art. Your options will be completely open, providing you with the freedom to choose.

The scope of art is expanding with new frontiers that offer opportunities never before imaginable. For example, new industries and manufacturing facilities need artists to imagine and invent advertising, products, tools, toys, fashions, graphics, and imagery on websites and soon the Metaverse. The ever-expanding need is why some colleges like Savannah College of Art and Design, Maryland Institute College of Art, and Ringling College of Art and Design have a dozen or more specialized majors in art, giving students the flexibility to adapt their program with new areas of interest.

Studying art will also keep you creative, allowing you to explore your evolving artistic style. Art is increasingly recognized as a valuable skill. If you are passionate about this pursuit, one day, your efforts will bear fruit!

The principle of true art is not to portray, but to evoke.

- Jerzy Kosinski

CHAPTER 4

ART & DESIGN
SUMMER PROGRAMS
& INTERNSHIPS
FOR HIGH SCHOOL
& COLLEGE STUDENTS

"Painting is easy when you don't know how, but very difficult when you do."

– Edgar Degas

S tart early to gain drawing, design, photography, and film experiences. Internships and summer programs are as important in your educational pathway as coursework. The lessons you learn from working collaboratively and collegially with other art and design-focused mentors may be different but equally important. Historian and scholar, W.E.B. DuBois (1868-1963), a founding member of the NAACP and the first Black American to earn a Ph.D. at Harvard said, "Education must not simply teach work - it must teach life." Your college, experiential, and life education go hand-in-hand, driven by purpose and foresight since life truly is a journey, not a destination.

WHY PARTICIPATE IN SUMMER PROGRAMS/INTERNSHIPS?

You should participate in summer programs and internships. While some students and parents chose these options to look good and show dedication, the real reason why you should participate is to develop your skills with critique and feedback from specialists in the field. Discussions, seminars, studio work, and portfolio development are immensely valuable for your future pursuits. However, merely living on a campus and getting a feel for what college would be like cannot be understated.

Note: This list is not exhaustive, and it is not an endorsement of any program. Dates, program descriptions, and program length may be changed from year to year.

SUMMER CAMPS & PROGRAMS FOR ART, DESIGN, FILM, PHOTOGRAPHY, AND ARCHITECTURE

Alabama

Auburn University – Architecture Camp – Creative Writing – Industrial Design

One week – Three Session Options – Full Scholarships Available (apply by April 1)

Students produce designs while working directly with professors.

Camp counselors support students with 24/7 questions, safety, and supervision.

Tuskegee University Taylor School of Architecture & Construction Science

Virtual Preview of Architecture and Construction at Tuskegee (V-PACT) 3-hour Virtual Program

Preview Architecture & Construction Science 2-Week Program

Arizona

Arcosanti – Re-Imagined Urbanism – 6-week discussion-based classes - AZ

Combining architecture and ecology (arcology), you can learn in the World's First Prototype Arcology.

Core values: (1) Frugality and Resourcefulness, (2) Ecological Accountability, (3) Experiential Learning, and (4) Leaving a Limited Footprint, Arcosanti is juxtaposed to mass consumerism, urban sprawl, unchecked consumption, and social isolation.

Arkansas

University of Arkansas – In Person & Virtual Design Camp – Fayetteville, AK

In-Person Grades 9-12 - design projects, studio groups, tours, & meetings with local designers.

No fee; completely remote; design camp lessons embedded; students are paired with a faculty member in a studio group.

Advanced Design Camp: students entering Grades 11-12, 2 weeks in Fayetteville

California

Academy of Art Institute – San Francisco

4-6 weeks – Advertising, Animation/VFX, Architecture, Fashion, Fine Art, Game Development, Graphic Design

Illustration, Industrial Design, Motion Pictures, Music Production, Photography, Writing for Film, TV, & Digital Media

California State Summer School of the Arts (CSSSA) – Sacramento, CA

Rigorous 4-week, pre-professional visual and performing arts 2D and 3D training program in painting, printmaking, sculpture, ceramics, digital media, and photography; scholarship possibility for CA residents. Grades 9 – 12.

Getty Museum – Paid Student Gallery Guide – Los Angeles, CA

Paid summer internship for teens ($2,400 in 2022). Learn the fundamentals of museums and public speaking while leading visitors around the grounds.

Also available – Open Call for teen photographers to share images, 8-week paid STEAM internship, and Summer Latin Academy at the Getty Villa to learn Latin.

Laguna College of Art & Design Pre-College Program – Laguna Beach, CA

Animation, Sculpture, Drawing Fundamentals, Figure Drawing, Graphic Design

Otis College of Art and Design Summer of Art – Los Angeles, CA

Intensive 4-week program for students 15+ for portfolio and studio training in architecture, conceptual art, digital media, graphic design, and printmaking, with lectures and critiques. Merit and need-based scholarships are available.

School of Creative & Performing Arts (SOCAPA) – Occidental College (13-18-year-olds)

2-week, 3-week - learn Filmmaking, Screenwriting, Dance, Music, Photography

SCI-Arc (Southern California Institute of Architecture) Immersive 4-week Summer Program (Design Immersion Days) – Los Angeles

Introduction to the academic and professional world of architecture – Grades 9-12

Stanford University – 8-Week Summer Courses and 3-Week Arts Institute

Architecture, Art, Drawing, Dance, Creative Writing, Music, and Photography

UCLA Summer Jumpstart Summer Art Inst, Digital Media Arts Inst., Digital Filmmaking Inst., Game Lab Inst.

2-week program - Portfolio development– credit available

Drawing, Painting, Photography, Sculpture, Video Art, Animation, and Game Design

USC Summer Film, Writing, and Architecture Programs – Los Angeles

2-4-week program, "Creative Writing Workshop", "Comedy Performance", "Exploration into Architecture"

Connecticut

Summer Studio: Discovering Graphic Design (AIGA) – Bridgeport, CT

Free 4-week hands-on program for Bridgeport rising juniors and seniors
Week 1 – Music Festival Poster, Week 2 – Digital Media Poster

Week 3 – Animating Your Ideas, Week 4 – Portfolio Art for College Applications

District of Columbia

Catholic University School of Architecture and Planning

Summer High School Program - 2-week Residential (Two Session Options)

George Washington University Digital Storytelling Pre-College Program – July

Produce stories with smartphones, learn storyboarding, and broadcast through social media

Craft ideas, capture images, & create compelling content, including character development

Georgetown University – 1-week – Creative Writing – Publishing

Fiction, Short Story, Poetry, and Professional Writing; visit literary hubs

Florida

Florida Atlantic University – Boca Raton, FL and Ft. Lauderdale, FL

School of Architecture – July (Three Session Options)

July 3-week program for rising sophomores, juniors, seniors, and students in their first 2 years of college - Portfolio development, fabrication, architectural education, portfolio display, critique

Certificate of Completion Awarded – Enrollment on a first-come, first-served basis

Ringling College of Art and Design – Sarasota, FL

Intensive 4-week program focused on art and design including computer animation, creative writing, digital sculpting, entertainment design, fabrication, film directing/production, game art, game design, illustration, painting, photography, storyboarding, and virtual reality development.

University of Florida Design Exploration Program (DEP)

3-week Residential Immersion into the architectural studio environment.

Construction of studio design projects, teamwork, seminars, field trips, architectural theory.

University of Miami Summer Scholars, Explorations in Architecture & Design– Coral Gables, FL

3-week Residential program; 6 college credits; Design, Graphics, and Theory.

Architecture, Landscape Architecture, Historic Preservation; Urban Planning.

Studio experience with drawing, model making, drafting, CAD, visual analysis.

Georgia

Emory University – Atlanta, GA – 2-, 4-, 6-Week Writing Programs

Journalism, Dramatic Writing, Media & Politics, Psychology & Fiction

Georgia Institute of Technology Pre-College Design Program – Atlanta, GA

2-week Residential program – College of Design – Grades 11 & 12 (Two Session Options)

Architecture, Building Construction, Industrial Design, and Music Technology

Savannah College of Art & Design – Savannah, GA - SCAD 5-week Rising Star & SCAD courses

2-week College of Design Residential program –– Grades 11 & 12 - Courses include Advertising, Animation, Virtual Reality, Illustration, Storyboarding, Photography, Painting, Fashion, Digital Film, Graphic Design, and Industrial Design

Illinois

Illinois Institute of Technology Summer Introduction to Architecture

2-week Experiment in Architecture for HS students – Comprehensive overview

1-week Exploration in Architecture for middle school students – studio-based, firm visits, field trips, projects.

Northwestern University – National HS Institute

5-week Film & Video, Music, Speech & Debate, Theatre

School of the Art Institute of Chicago – Early College Program for HS Students

1-, 2-, 4-week Residential programs in Painting, Drawing, Animation, Comics/Graphic Novels, and Fashion Design.

Portfolio development programs; earn college credit. Full-tuition scholarships are available.

Southern Illinois University Carbondale – Kid Architecture

1-week Elementary Grades, Middle School & High School Architecture Camp

University of Illinois at Chicago Architecture - HiArch Summer High School Program

1-, 2-week (July) - HS students are introduced to the culture of architecture, design, thinking, and making.

University of Chicago Creative Writing Immersion

"Collegiate Writing: Awakening Into Consciousness" and "Creative Writing: Fiction"

Indiana

University of Notre Dame Summer Scholars Program

2-weeks HS Students – Film, Photography, Performing Arts - studios, seminars, and field trips

Iowa

Iowa State University – College of Design - HS Design Camps

1-week HS Students – Architecture, Studio/Fine Arts, Graphic Design, Interior Design, & Industrial Design

Maryland

Maryland Institute College of Art (MICA) – Baltimore, MD

2-, 3-, 5-week HS Students – Live instruction, studio time, workshops, artist talks, collaboration, feedback, critique, evaluation

Massachusetts

Boston College - Boston, MA – Creative Writing Seminar Program

3-week (July) Residential Program – HS Students – nonfiction, fiction, poetry – hone techniques

Create & edit the class literary journal and present writings at a public reading

Harvard University GSD Design Discovery– Cambridge, MA (Ages 18-mid-career professionals)

3-week Residential Program – Architecture, Landscape, Urban Planning & Design

Physical modeling, fabrication, assembly

Harvard Summer Program for High School Students

2-week non-credit program; 7-week college credit program (live in campus dorms)

Credit classes include: Creating Comics & Graphic Novels; Drawing & the Digital Age; Advertising, Landscape, & Visual Imagery; Creative Writing

Massachusetts College of Art & Design – 4-Week Art Immersion Program

Students take 3 foundation courses; closing exhibition

Massachusetts Institute of Technology – Urbaneframe – Cambridge, MA

HS Students - Summer Design-Build Project

CAD, drafting, sketching, mapping and context study, historical research, carpentry & construction

Tufts University – 6-Week Writing Intensive

Writing exercises, evaluation from professors, revise, develop papers that build on a theme

University of Massachusetts Amherst Pre-College – Amherst, MA

1-, 2-, 3-week Residential Intensives Grades 10-12

3-D Design, 3-D Animation, Building & Construction Technology; Combatting the Climate Crisis

Summer Engineering Institute, Summer Design Academy, Programming for Aspiring Scientists

Wellesley College – Wellesley, MA

2-week Residential Program - EXPLO Pre-College + Career for Grades 10-12

Three session options; Topics include – AI, Entrepreneurship, Engineering, Medicine, Law, CSI

Youth Design Boston (AIGA) – Boston, MA

Summer Graphic Design Internship & Mentoring Program

Michigan

Andrews University School of Architecture & Interior Design - Renaissance Kids – Berrien Springs, MI

Virtual Studio Projects; lecture; community build projects

Interlochen Center for the Arts – Summer Arts Camp – 1-6 Weeks

Creative Writing, Dance, Art, Motion Picture, Music, Theatre, Visual Arts

University of Michigan – Stamps School of Art & Design – BFA Preview

3-week (June/July)– HS Students – Creative retreat with state-of-the-art facilities & museum excursions

Missouri

Washington University in St. Louis – Creative Writing Institute and HS Summer Scholars Program

2-week program – fiction, nonfiction, and poetry; morning writer's workshops – editing and sharing work

5-8 week – Dance, Journalism, Photography, Music, Drama, Photojournalism

University of Missouri Kansas City – Department of Architecture, Urban Planning & Design MA

Design Discovery Program – Architecture, Interior Design, Landscape Architecture

3-day (July) Non-Residential Program – HS Students/Current College Students

Nebraska

University of Nebraska College of Architecture – Lincoln, NE

6-day (June) Residential Program – Grades 11 & 12 – Studio training; architectural design; scholarships

New Jersey

New Jersey Institute of Technology – Hillier College of Architecture & Design

1-week (July) Residential Program – HS Students – Architecture, Interior Design, Industrial Design, Digital Design

Summer Architecture + Design Programs (2 Start Dates)

New York

AIA New York – Center for Architecture

1-week (July) Residential Program – HS Students – Architecture

Programs for Grades 3-12 include Architectural Design Studio, Drawing Architecture, Rooftop Dwelling, Dream House, Treehouses, Skyscrapers, Green Island Home, Subway Architecture, Waterfront City, Parks & Playground Design, and Neighborhood Design

Columbia University - New York, NY – Summer Immersion

3-week July-August Residential Program – Architecture, Creative Writing, Drawing, Filmmaking, Photography, Theater, or Visual Arts

Cooper Union - New York, NY – Summer Art Intensive

4-week July-August Residential Programs – Portfolio Development, Exhibition, Anthology Publication

Animation, Creative Writing, Photography, Drawing, Graphic Design, & Stop Animation

Cornell University – Ithaca, NY – Precollege Studies and 3-Week Transmedia: Image, Sound, Motion Program

3-, 6-, 9-week June-August Residential Program; Drawing and New Media (collage, drawing, digital photography, screen printing, & video)

Architecture: Design Studio, Culture, and Society, Architectural Science & Technology

New York University Summer Art Intensive

4-week Immersive program in Digital & Video, Sculpture, or Visual Arts

Parsons School of Design – New York and Paris

4-week - Online and on-campus summer programs for students from 3rd grade to 12th

NYC - Portfolio building in 3-credit immersive Design, Studio Art, Photography, Illustration, Game Design

Paris Program – Design & Mgmt, Explorations in Drawing & Painting, Fashion Design

Rensselaer Polytechnic University – Troy, NY

Architecture Career Discovery Program

School of Creative & Performing Arts (SOCAPA) – New York (13-18-year-olds)

2-, 3-week - Learn Filmmaking, Screenwriting, Dance, Music, Photography

Sotheby's Summer Institute – Pre-College, Undergrad, Graduate, and Professional

New York, London, and Virtual Programs

Intensives in Painting & Drawing, Curating, Luxury Marketing, Art Crime/Art Law, Fashion, and Art Business

Syracuse University – Syracuse, NY – On-Campus and Online Programs for HS Students

2-, 3-, 6-week programs 3-D Studio Art; Sculpture; Architecture; Design Studies; Writing Immersion

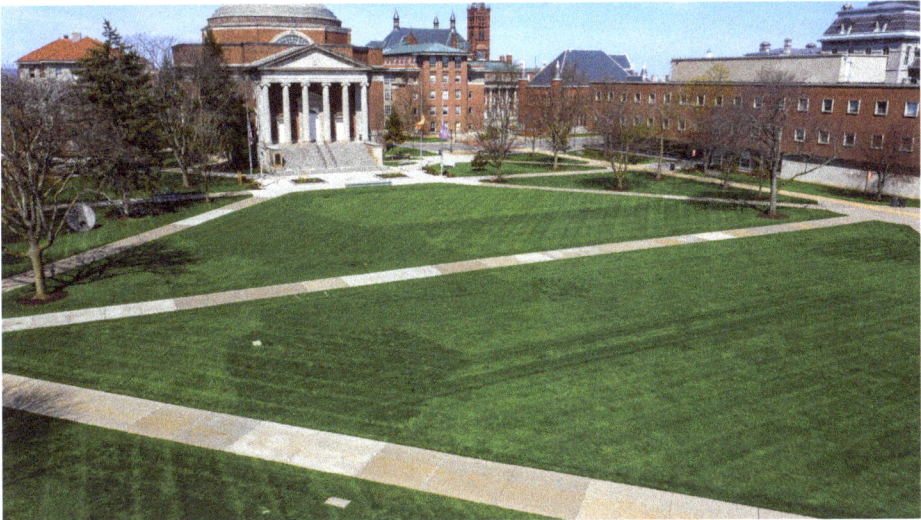

Oklahoma

University of Oklahoma Architecture Summer Academy

1-week (June) Residential Program – HS Students – Architecture, Interior Design, Construction Science

Design in Action: Creativity, Innovation, and Sustainability Shaping the Built Environment

Pennsylvania

Carnegie Mellon University Pre-College Art Program - Pittsburgh, PA

3-, 4-, 6-week (July-August) Residential Program – Intensive Studio Studies Portfolio development in Drawing, Sculpture, Animation, and Concept Studio Art Chestnut Hill College Global Solutions Lab

Interactive Global Simulation, Electrifying Africa, & UN Sustainable Development Goals

1-week programs – HS Students – Intensive collaborative team solutions to big problems

Drexel University Westphal College of Media Arts & Design – Discovering Architecture

2-week Residential Program – HS Students – Intensive Studio Architecture Program

Visit prominent architectural, multi-disciplinary design offices; meet architects

Maywood University Pre-College Summer Workshop School of Architecture

2-week (July) Residential Program – HS Students – Design Your Future Architecture Program

Pennsylvania State University Architecture & Landscape Architecture Summer Camp

1-week (July) – HS Students –Architecture, Graphics, Design, and the Built Environment Program

Temple University Tyler School of Art and Architecture Pre-College Architecture Program

Architecture Institute – Philadelphia, PA

2-week (July-August) Residential Program – HS Students – Studio Architecture

Rhode Island

Brown University – 1-4 Weeks – Art Themed Courses

Creative Writing, Music, Studio Art, Art History

Rhode Island School of Design Pre-College School of Design – Providence, RI

6-week (June-July) Residential Program – HS Students – Foundational Art & Design Studies

Figure drawing, projects, trips, exhibitions

Roger Williams University High School Summer Academy in Architecture

4-week (July-August) Residential Program – Grades 11 & 12 – Explore Studio Architecture

Seminars, fieldwork, studio, portfolio development

South Carolina

Clemson University Pre-College School of Architecture Program

1-week (July-August) Residential Program – Grades 7-12

Engineering Design, Mechanical Engineering, Civil Engineering, Intelligent Vehicles, Materials Engineering

Tennessee

The University of Memphis Discovering Architecture + Design

1-day – HS Students – Design programs on architecture, interior design, and the built environment

The University of Tennessee, Knoxville College of Architecture + Design

1-week UT Summer Design Camp (July) Residential – HS Students

Immersive architecture, graphic design, and professional practice program

Vanderbilt Summer Academy – Nashville, TN – 3-Week Program

"Digital Storytelling", "Writing Fantasy Fiction", "Math & Music", "Writing Short Stories"

Texas

Texas Tech Anson L Clark Scholars Program – Research Area: Advertising, Architecture, Art, Dance, or Theatre

7-week – Grades 11 & 12 – Residential Program (must be 17 years old by start date) – no program fee

Intensive research-based program; $500 meal card; $750 tax-free stipend

University of Houston & Wonderworks Pre-College Summer Discovery Program

Hines College of Architecture & Design – Introduction to Architecture

6-week – HS Students – Design programs with hands-on studio, field trips, and portfolio workshop

The University of Texas at Austin Summer Design Camps – 2-D Game Design, 3-D Game Design, 3-D Animation/Motion

School of Design and Creative Technologies

1-week – HS Students – portfolio development and design

Vermont

School of Creative & Performing Arts (SOCAPA) – Burlington, VT (13-18-year-olds)

2-week, 3-week - learn Filmmaking, Screenwriting, Dance, Music, Photography

Virginia

Virginia Commonwealth University (VCUArts) Pre-College

3-Week On-Campus Program Course Options – 2D Portfolio Development, Photography,

Clay: More Than Just Mud, Sketchbook to Controller, Animation Workshop, Sculptural Forms,

Jewelry Making, Fashion Design, Stage Combat, Musical Theatre, Acting From Page to Stage

Virginia Tech Inside Architecture + Design

1-week – HS Students – Hands-on design studio architecture program

Washington

DigiPen Academy – K-12 Animation, Film, Music, Game Design Summer Programs – Redmond, WA

1-week and 2-week programs, including Teen Art & Animation; Film Scoring

Music & Sound Design; Video Game Development; Animation Masterclass

University of Washington – Seattle, WA – Middle and HS Students

1-Week - Neurotechnology Young Scholars Program, DawgBytes Computer Science Camp,

Material Science Camp, and Summer Session Art Classes

Wisconsin

The University of Wisconsin Milwaukee School of Architecture & Urban Planning

1-week – HS Students – Design program on architecture, interior design, and the built environment

TAKE ADVANTAGE OF THIS TIME TO EXPLORE

During high school and college, you have the opportunity to explore your interests through summer programs, skill-building camps, and internships. Try out different fields you might not have considered before. You never really have the same chance to consider alternatives in quite the same way. Learn something new. There are hundreds of career areas you may never have considered. Have some fun while you are at it!

Everything has its beauty, but not everyone sees it.

– Andy Warhol

CHAPTER 5

UNIVERSITY OPTIONS: EXCELLENT COLLEGE PROGRAMS FOR DRAWING & PAINTING

"Creativity is contagious, pass it on."

– Albert Einstein

I n the United States, more than 300 colleges offer a 4-year accredited bachelor's degree in fine arts. Altogether, more than two million people in the United States have degrees in visual and performing arts, with about half specifically in visual arts. However, only about ten percent make the bulk of their income through art.

U.S. College Students – approximately 19.6 million

> 14.5 million attending public colleges

> 5.14 million attending private colleges

> 2,679 4-year colleges; 1,303 2-year colleges

Another interesting statistic is that undergraduate enrollment dropped more than 4% from fall 2019 to fall 2020 and another 3.5% from fall 2020 to fall 2021, representing approximately a 1,500,000 loss of students during the pandemic. However, with test-optional admissions opening the door to more students without test scores or who test poorly, more students applied to the top schools.

TOP SIXTEEN PAINTING PROGRAMS

1. Yale University
2. Rhode Island School of Design
3. School of the Art Inst. of Chicago
4. Columbia University
5. Bard College
6. Boston University
7. Maryland Institute College of Art
8. University of California, Los Angeles
9. California Institute of the Arts
10. Hunter College - CUNY
11. Pratt Institute
12. School of Visual Arts
13. Virginia Commonwealth University
14. Cranbrook Academy of Art
15. Temple University
16. Rutgers University

Everyone has heard about the top colleges in fine arts. Yet, there are many more excellent programs. The colleges that offer **the most bachelor's degrees in Fine Art** each year are:

1. School of the Art Inst. of Chicago
2. Cal State Fullerton
3. Cal State Long Beach
4. University of North Texas
5. City University of New York
6. Florida State University
7. University of Central Florida
8. San Jose State University
9. Indiana University - IUPUI
10. Hunter College - CUNY

U.S. – ACCREDITED COLLEGES FOCUSED ON ART

United States

Art Academy of Cincinnati (OH)

ArtCenter College of Design (CA)

Art Institute of Boston (MA)

Art Institute of Pittsburgh (PA)

California College of the Arts (CA)

California Institute of the Arts (CA)

Cleveland Institute of Art (OH)

College for Creative Studies (MI)

Columbia College Chicago (IL)

Cooper Union (NY)

Corcoran Col. of Art & Design - GWU (DC)

Cornish College of the Arts (WA)

Fashion Institute of Technology (NY)

Kansas City Art Institute (MO)

Kendall College of Art & Design (MI)

Laguna College of Art & Design (CA)

Lyme Academy College of Fine Arts (CT)

Maine College of Art (ME)

Maryland Institute College of Art (MD)

Mass. College of Art & Design (MA)

Memphis College of Art (TN)

Milwaukee Institute of Art & Design (WI)

Minneapolis College of Art & Design (MN)

Montserrat College of Art (MA)

Moore College of Art & Design (PA)

New Hampshire Institute of Art (NH)

N. Michigan Univ. School of Art & Design (MI)

Oregon College of Art & Craft (OR)

Otis College of Art & Design (CA)

Pacific Northwest College of Art (OR)

Parsons School of Design (NY)

Pratt Institute (NY)

Rhode Island School of Design (RI)

Ringling College of Art & Design (FL)

San Francisco Art Institute (CA)

Savannah College of Art & Design (GA)

School of the Art Institute of Chicago (IL)

School of the Museum of Fine Arts (MA)

Vermont College of Fine Arts (VT)

Watkins College of Art, Design, & Film (TN)

You might even want to study drawing and painting abroad. Though international programs are not profiled in this book, some of the best are included in the following lists.

U.S. – ACCREDITED COLLEGES FOCUSED ON ART

International

Adelaide Central School of Art (Australia)

Alberta University of the Arts (Canada)

Bauhaus University Weimar (Germany)

Camberwell College of Arts (England)

Emily Carr Univ. of Art & Design (Canada)

Government College of Art & Craft (India)

Grekov Odessa Art School (Ukraine)

National Art School (Australia)

Nova Scotia College of Art & Design Univ. (Canada)

Ontario College of Art & Design Univ. (Canada)

Paris College of Art (France)

2021 QS RANKED TOP UNIVERSITIES FOR ART AND DESIGN WORLDWIDE

1. Royal College of Art (U.K.)
2. University of the Arts London (U.K.)
3. Parsons School of Design (NY-USA)
4. Rhode Island School of Design (RI-USA)
5. Massachusetts Institute of Technology (MA-USA)
6. Politecnico de Milano (Italy)
7. Aalto University (Finland)
8. School of the Art Institute of Chicago (IL-USA)
9. Glasgow School of Art (U.K.)
10. Pratt Institute (NY-USA)
11. ArtCenter (CA-USA)
12. Delft University of Technology (Netherlands)
13. Design Academy Eindhoven (Netherlands)
14. Tongji University (China)
15. Goldsmiths, University of London (U.K.)
16. Royal Melbourne Institute of Technology (Australia)
17. California Institute of the Arts (CA-USA)
18. Carnegie Mellon University (PA-USA)
19. Stanford University (CA-USA)
20. Hong Kong Polytechnic University (H.K. SAR)

Although this book only profiles a fraction of the art schools and only those U.S. colleges with bachelor's degree programs in drawing, painting, and fine arts, there are undoubtedly many schools with excellent faculty and facilities, some even in your local area.

SPOTLIGHT ON 5 NON-NEW YORK CITY PROGRAMS

Bard College (private, Annandale-on-Hudson, NY)

B.A. in Studio Arts

Bard College is a small liberal arts school between New York City and Albany. Its mission is to serve the community while supporting free speech, scholarship, and rigorous inquiry. With a campus that overlooks the Hudson River and the Catskill Mountains, the college has an enrollment of approximately 1,800 undergraduates, 600 graduate students, 1,200 in early college programs, and 2,500 in Bard's global affiliates.

Bard's Division of the Arts includes a studio arts program, developing the visual language, technique, and self-introspection. Students take art history along with courses from drawing, painting, printmaking, digital design, and media. Students culminate their program by producing a senior project presented at an exhibition. Students who need funds may take part in the Fund for Visual Learning for supplies and senior project grants.

Bard's specialized International BA program (IBA) is unique in that it goes beyond study abroad to allow students to immerse themselves in multiple cultures with students around the globe. Students participate in three semesters away from the campus on language intensive trips, short-term study away programs, or international exchanges. Bard also has a focused Bard Globalization and International Affairs program in New York City.

George Washington University (private, Washington, D.C.)

BFA Fine Arts

Students at GW can earn a BFA in fine arts focused on drawing and surface, form and materials, time and light, and interaction. Additional courses are offered in ceramics, painting, drawing, photography, printmaking, sculpture, and time-based media. With studios across the street from the White House, there is no better access to opportunities for inspiration. Furthermore, the subway line station is near the center of the GW campus so getting anywhere in the D.C. metropolitan area is fast.

When GW acquired the Corcoran School of the Arts & Design, multidisciplinary opportunities grew within Washington, D.C.'s natural training ground. With access to numerous internships, many of them paid, students cultivate their careers while pushing the bounds of all forms of art. Furthermore, the faculty are some of the most outstanding in the field.

GW offers the Corcoran Scholars Program, which provides funding for top students who are continuously enrolled based on academics and the submission of a portfolio. The award is renewable for up to 10 consecutive semesters.

Northern Arizona University (public, Flagstaff, AZ)

BFA Painting

NAU's art major, focused on painting, in the School of Art offers hands-on experience nestled in a fascinating landscape of mountains and Native American tribes. The location is nearby seven major national parks with numerous cultural influences. NAU educates future painters using oil, water-based, and alternative media. You will leave a mark on the world while expanding the possibilities of your art through courses in business practices, grant applications, gallery representation, self-promotion, and creating a contemporary studio.

Students learn commercial art skills as well as training in art education, gallery work, and mural development. Courses teach materials, methods, techniques, canvas stretching, paint mixing, glazing, varnishing, light, shadow, composition, and color theory. NAU has a number of galleries and an art museum.

Seattle University (private, Seattle, WA)
BA Visual Art

Seattle U's BA in visual art allows students to explore various modes of 2-D, 3-D, and 4-D disciplines. While embedded in a liberal arts school, the BA is a degree focused on having students discover their artistic voice within the university's vibrant community. The classes are small and incoming students form a cohort with mentors and a supportive learning environment. Students can concentrate in painting and drawing, printmaking, ceramics, 3-D design, and sculpture. Seattle University also offers an honors program for those who are interested.

Students do not need to submit a portfolio in the application process. At the end of a student's sophomore year, they will present their work to the faculty. Students have access to internships, and many continue on to earn an MFA. The program culminates in an exhibition of works in the Vachon Gallery.

Syracuse University (private, Syracuse, NY)
BA Fine Arts, minor Painting; BFA Illustration

SU's College of Arts and Sciences offers cutting-edge tools and opportunities in fine arts while SU's School of Visual and Performing Arts offers a focused BFA degree in illustration with skill-building in drawing, painting, digital media, and research. Students can focus on character development, editorial, sequential, and products. Meanwhile, students in the College of Arts and Sciences become grounded in hands-on training while gaining a liberal arts education at the same time. Syracuse also offers more than 100 study abroad programs in 60 countries, with short and long-term options. SU's London design program is excellent. However, SU also offers a MAYmester session in Museums and Contemporary Practices in New York City or Washington, D.C.

THE MANY ROADS TO ARTISTIC SUCCESS

There are numerous ways you can be successful in drawing and painting. The training you get in college can be immensely valuable, particularly while being surrounded by highly skilled practitioners in the art. There is no one road to get to your goal, just as there is not one goal you may want to achieve. Skills in drawing and painting offer numerous pathways and byways. Some famous artists attended smaller programs where they gained a broader or more extensive liberal arts education. Others never went to college at all. Exposure to the many different forms of art with students who have diverse interests cannot be understated. Whichever road you take, enjoy the journey.

Two roads diverged in a wood, and I took the one less traveled by,
And that has made all the difference.

- Robert Frost

CHAPTER 6

WHAT IS THE DIFFERENCE BETWEEN AN AA, AS, BA, BS, BFA, AND MFA?

"Painting is just another way of keeping a diary."

– **Pablo Picasso**

UNDERGRADUATE AND GRADUATE DEGREES

AA – Associate of Arts – 2-year degree

AS – Associate of Science – 2-year degree

BA – Bachelor of Arts – 4-year degree

BS – Bachelor of Science – 4-year degree

BFA – Bachelor of Fine Arts – 4-year degree with most classes focused on art

MFA – Master of Fine Arts – 1-2-year degree earned after the BA, BS, or BFA

Basically, BA and BS degrees are degrees that typically offer a liberal arts foundation along with a major or concentration in a specific subject. Meanwhile, a BFA is considered a professional arts-focused degree with fewer courses in English, science, math, social science, and the humanities. Thus, the BFA is a specialist qualification in the arts. A BA or BS degree in fine arts is also valuable. The BFA is more focused on the specific area of art you choose.

The BA and BS degrees include significantly more liberal arts classes and thus are more general degrees. However, the intention of the BFA degree is for students to pursue an arts-focused curriculum, and thus there are fewer general subject courses.

Finally, while many AA or AS degrees are focused on providing technical or professional skills, an AA or AS in these areas are often interchangeable. However, a BFA may be seen as different since there is typically more coursework focused on your specific pursuit, and thus, you may have more technical experiences and knowledge than someone who has a BA or BS.

AA – ASSOCIATE OF ARTS

The Associate of Arts degree is typically a 2-year general studies degree offered online or in-person by a community college. However, some universities offer AA degrees as well. Often, the Associate of Arts degree focused on the liberal arts has no barrier to entry, meaning that students can enter most AA programs with a high school diploma or the equivalent. Some students take a longer or shorter time to complete the AA based upon their skills upon entering the program, certainty about the direction they are heading, and the transfer requirements for the program they desire. For example, students majoring in business may have additional business, communication, accounting, and economics requirements and need to create an academic plan early in their program to finish in two years.

AS – ASSOCIATE OF SCIENCE

The Associate of Science degree is very similar to the AA. However, the AS degree frequently emphasizes science and math and often has additional requirements.

BA – BACHELOR OF ARTS

The Bachelor of Arts degree is typically a 4-year degree offered online or in-person by a college or university. However, a few community colleges offer BA degrees as well. Some students complete their BA in fewer years depending upon AP/IB credit, dual enrollment in high school, and summer/intersession classes. College programs have stricter or less stringent requirements depending upon the school. The Bachelor of Arts degree frequently requires students to take lower-division (first and second year) liberal arts courses before taking specialized courses focused around a major or concentration in their third and fourth years.

The time required to earn a BA depends upon each student's skills and advanced placement credit when entering the program. Some students change the direction they are heading and their chosen major which can add more time. According to the National Center for Educational Statistics, college advisors aid students in finishing "on time" though less than half of all students in the United States who start a BA program do not finish their degree in four years.[1]

---

1   IEC NCES, "Digest of Education Statistics, Table 326.10," IES NCES, n.d., https://nces.ed.gov/programs/digest/d20/tables/dt20_326.10.asp?referer=raceindica.asp

BS – BACHELOR OF SCIENCE

The Bachelor of Science degree is very similar to the BA. However, the BS degree frequently emphasizes science and math and often has additional requirements.[2]

BFA – BACHELOR OF FINE ARTS

The Bachelor of Fine Arts is a 4-year college degree focusing on the arts. BFA students are often not required to take as many English, science, math, social science, and humanities courses. However, they must still complete roughly the same number of credits as a person who earns a BA or BS, and the courses are not necessarily easier. BFA students frequently take general art requirements to lay a foundation in drawing, graphic design, and courses in their specialty area during their first two years, along with basic writing and quantitative skill-building.

BFA students are traditionally art-in-practice students who learn the technical craft of their art form while putting in enormous numbers of hours practicing their skill doing assignments and participating in internships and experiential learning. Students who know that they want a future in the arts often find this avenue perfectly tailored for their pursuits. However, students who change their minds and

2   IEC NCES, "Digest of Education Statistics, Table 326.10," IES NCES, n.d., https://nces.ed.gov/programs/digest/d20/tables/dt20_326.10.asp?referer=raceindica.asp

transfer to a university in another degree program may require an additional year to make up for coursework they have not completed.

MFA – MASTER OF FINE ARTS

The Master of Fine Arts is a graduate degree for students who have completed their BA, BS, or BFA. This degree takes one to two years depending upon the program, coursework, and experiential component, which may be a capstone, practicum, internship, or thesis. While there are also MA and MS degrees, many art students who continue to earn their master's degree in the arts chose to focus on their field of interest. The MFA is an intensive immersion into a higher level of skill-building. However, students who graduate with an MFA have a broader range of talents and experiences than those who earn their bachelor's degrees. While admission into these programs is generally selective, with planning, preparation, and a good portfolio, there are options for you to pursue your interests.

THE SEVEN MAJOR DIFFERENCES BETWEEN THE ASSOCIATE, BACHELORS, AND MASTER'S DEGREES

1. Starting Point
2. Academic Discipline
3. Time to Completion
4. Location of the Education
5. Educational Costs
6. Earning Power
7. Professional Opportunities

STARTING POINT

Most students who begin with an Associate of Arts (AA) or Associate of Science (AS) have no college credits. Starting from scratch with their college education, they accumulate their 60+ units beginning from this community college starting point. While most students earn AA or AS degrees at a community college, some earn this degree at a 4-year college or university.

The AA or AS is either a terminal degree, meaning that the student will not continue on with their bachelor's degree or just a steppingstone to their BA, BS, or BFA. The difference between the associate's and bachelor's degrees is just the starting point.

The starting point for students who pursue a bachelor's degree may be farther along the traditional 4-year pathway. Meanwhile, the starting point for the master's degree (MA, MS, or MFA) begins after obtaining a bachelor's degree.

ACADEMIC DISCIPLINE

Every degree encompasses different requirements. Requirements for the AA differ from an AS. Similarly, the requirements for the BA, BS, and BFA also differ. With two additional years of coursework, the BA, BS, and BFA are more thorough. The MA, MS, and MFA build upon the bachelor's degree and even deeper. Students studying painting will not take the same classes as those pursuing graphic design, though some may overlap. While both are essential to the fine arts, the necessary skills for each career area are distinct. Thus, the course requirements are also unique.

Furthermore, with the myriad of combinations, it is rare that any two undergraduate students have the same exact classes in the same exact order. Since the requirements for a chemistry degree are not the same as for biology and a degree in illustration differs from, for example, photography, the course requirements for different majors may include different numbers of credits as well as different classes and competencies.

TIME TO COMPLETION

Associate of Arts (AA) and Associate of Science (AS) degrees typically take two years, while most BA, BS, and BFA degrees are 4-year programs, depending upon full-time or part-time status. Students who transfer in credits or earn credits otherwise can reduce their time to completion.

Some students may choose to extend their education in drawing and painting by earning a second bachelor's degree in another field. By cross-training in graphic design, photography, or marketing, students open more doors. Additionally, a degree in business on the bachelor's level or Master's in Business Administration (MBA) may lead to alternative leadership positions.

Time in college can be reduced. Some students enter a BA, BS, or BFA program having already completed college credits because they were dual-enrolled or they took college classes directly through a college or university ahead of time. Some students have taken AP/ IB tests from taking higher-level classes while in high school and earned qualifying scores to be granted credits by the college or university. Other ways students can enter at a different starting point are with credit-by-exam, CLEP tests, experiential credits, and those granted in the military.

Colleges and universities are keenly aware of the challenges students face today with work, illness, and family responsibilities. Thus, many schools of higher education offer flexible enrollment with opportunities for part-time, evening, weekend, and online classes.

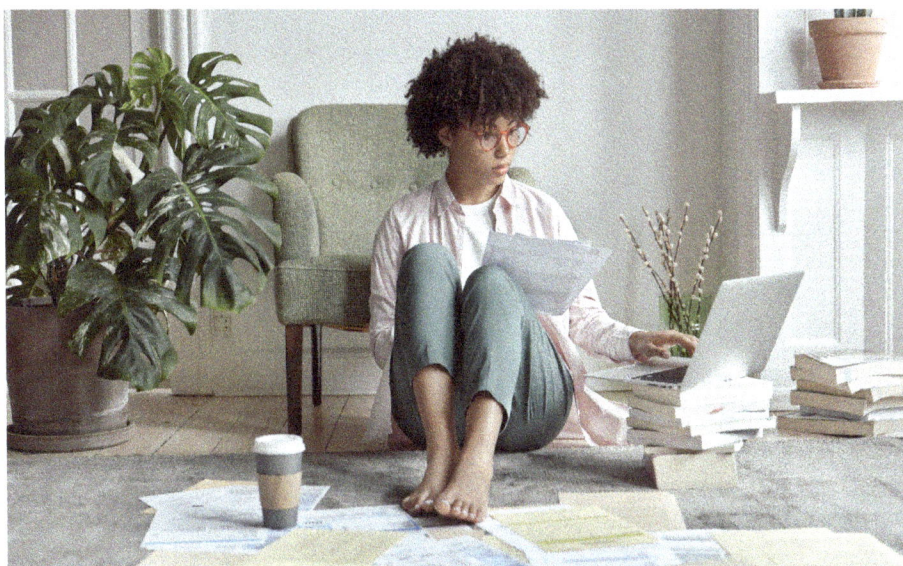

LOCATION OF THE EDUCATION

The AA and AS are earned at colleges that grant 2-year degrees. The location may be at a local community college or a university. BA, BS, and BFA programs are offered at a 4-year college or university. However, with online classes, students have the flexibility to take classes from colleges farther away as well. Thus, the location in which a typical student studies is not as set as it once was. Nevertheless, the in-person internships are often situated in corporate hubs and thus require grounding to a specific location.

EDUCATIONAL COSTS

Since the AA or AS requires a shorter amount of time and is typically completed at a lower-cost community college, the cost for an associate's degree is typically less than a bachelor's degree. Master's degree programs cost more per credit but take less time than a bachelor's degree.

On the other hand, many students can obtain financial aid in the form of grants, loans, and both merit and need-based scholarships. This aid can pay for school and reduce debt after college.

EARNING POWER

Students with more education can earn more. According to the 2019 National Center for Educational Statistics (NCES) average income data for the median person based on degree attainment,[3]

Master's Degree or Higher - $70,000

Bachelor's Degree - $55,700

Associate's Degree - $43,300

High School - $35,000

Of course, there is a wide range in annual salaries from those who have consistent work and are paid six-digit or seven-digit salaries to those who work one or two paid shows per year and earn less than $20,000. Thus, the average seems low when the variation is huge.

---

3   IES NCES, "Annual Earnings by Educational Attainment," IEC NCES, May 2021, https://nces.ed.gov/programs/coe/indicator/cba

PROFESSIONAL OPPORTUNITIES

Earning a BA, BS, or BFA opens more doors than an AA or AS. Similarly, an MA, MS, or MFA opens more doors than a BA, BS, or BFA. Baccalaureate and master's degrees require more training. You can obtain this training through workshops or studio classes, but with a scholarship to pay for college, you might find that the training and opportunities are worth your time. Besides, you will gain additional skills that could prove valuable in your future.

The beautiful thing about learning is that no one can take it from you.

- B.B. King

CHAPTER 7

COLLEGE ADMISSIONS: APPLICATIONS, ESSAYS, RECOMMENDATIONS, AND FINANCIAL AID

"A picture is a poem without words."

– Horace

R ISD, SVA, Cal Arts, NYU, and SAIC stand out for drawing and painting with amazing faculty, excellent facilities, and easy access to internships. While most students consider New York City for the top college art programs and internships, they should not discount other major metropolitan areas like Chicago and Los Angeles as well as cities around the country that are meccas for artists and journalists. However, you cannot go wrong going to RISD for its deep dive into the world of art. These colleges offer a rigorous course of study and socially responsible projects on the cutting edge of art, design, and forward-thinking optimism.

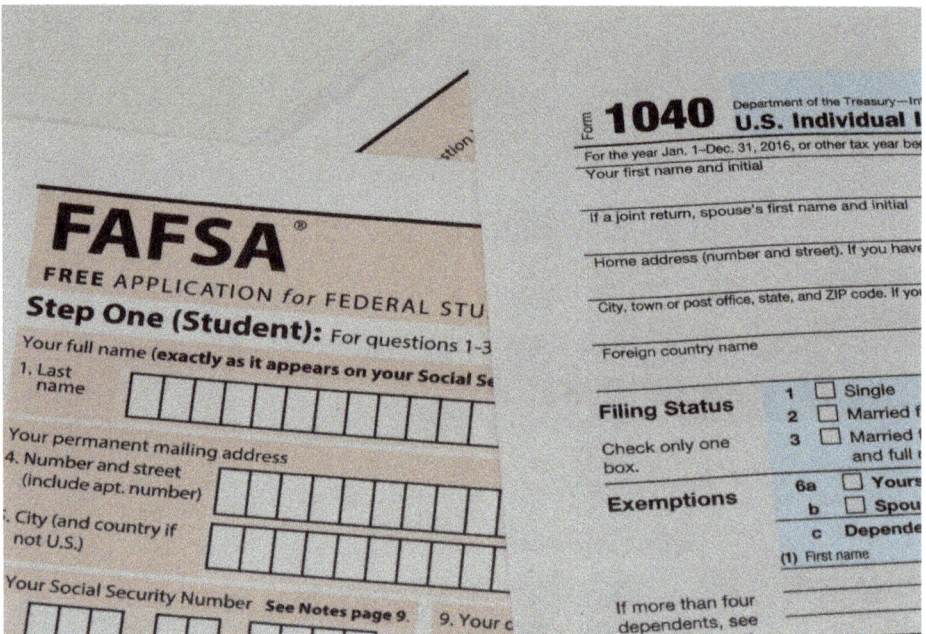

FINANCIAL AID

Nearly every university in the United States offers money for college. These funds come in the form of grants/scholarships that do not need to be paid back, loans that need to be repaid, and 'work study', where you are paid for a job associated with the college or university. The grants or scholarships are either need-based or merit-based. Need-based means that the college or government determines that, based on your income, you will be unable to attend without additional resources. Merit-based means that the college or university is offering you money based on some combination of your grades, test scores, skills, and/or talent.

To obtain need-based financial aid, almost all colleges require you to submit the Free Application for Federal Student Aid (FAFSA) found at www.studentaid.gov. Some colleges also require the College Scholarship Service (CSS) Profile which is available on the College Board website at www.collegeboard. org. Both the FAFSA and CSS Profile require your income based upon the tax returns you file with the U.S. federal government.

Most people will be able to download the tax information directly into the FAFSA form using the Data Retrieval Tool (DRT). This automatic process not only saves time, but the DRT also ensures that the correct information goes into the right locations on the form. Check anyway afterward since there could be an error. If your family has not filed a tax return yet, you can estimate the amounts. However, all income and other financial information will eventually need to be verified for you to receive need-based aid.

SCHOLARSHIPS

Merit scholarships offered through a college or university that are based upon academic success or may not have additional forms and essays to complete. Merit scholarships based upon talent typically require a portfolio, performance, audition, or some other demonstration of your skills. Check your art, dance, music, writing, theatre, research, robotics, engineering, or program to see what the college requires. Note: Each college or university has a different set of rules for what and how you submit your art, video, writing samples, or other demonstration of your mastery.

Please check out the profile section at the back of this book for scholarships and requirements. Additionally, look up the college website for their financial aid process. To help you get a sense of available scholarships, I selected six schools at random from the options listed in the profile section.

ArtCenter College of Design

ArtCenter offers more than $22 million in scholarships for students with need and talent each year. Amounts vary based on need, talent, available funds, and recommendations from the scholarship committee. ArtCenter offers continuing scholarships for students currently in school. ArtCenter awards also scholarships to support diverse students. Additionally, ArtCenter offers approximately twenty other donor-sponsored scholarships.

Columbia College Chicago

Columbia College offers merit and need-based scholarships to more than a hundred freshmen, transfer, and graduate students. Most of the scholarships are renewable each year with given GPA and coursework requirements. Columbia College meets four years of full-need of both domestic and international applicants. For merit scholarships, creative samples must be submitted with the application. Full tuition awards are also available.

Pratt Institute

Pratt offers generous merit-based scholarships. Sixty percent of incoming first-year students are offered merit-based awards for their talent. In addition, Pratt has restricted and endowed scholarships along with its need-based financial aid program. International students are also eligible for merit-based awards. No additional application is required for prospective students; all admitted students are considered automatically.

Rhode Island School of Design

RISD offers scholarships to students who demonstrate academic and talent-based success and financial need. Many students receive $20,000 awards. However, scholarships are need-based, and international students must pay the full tuition.

Savannah College of Art and Design (SCAD)

Some colleges are exceptionally generous with money for a large proportion of students. For example, at SCAD, 80% of new applicants receive merit & need-based scholarships. These opportunities are available for U.S. citizens, permanent residents, and international students.

Syracuse University

Syracuse University students received more than $400 million in financial aid. Syracuse offers internal merit-based scholarships and supports students in finding external funds as well. Merit-based funding is offered to more than 35% of the incoming class. Approximately 80% of SU's incoming students received some type of financial support. Syracuse University offers a financial aid package to incoming students that meet full-need.

PRIVATE SCHOLARSHIPS

Some scholarship money available does not come directly from the college. Private individuals, corporations, and endowments offer outside scholarships for students who apply. Some of these scholarships are significant. A few offer full tuition. Here are a few of the thousands to consider.

Gates Millennium Scholarship

Full scholarships are granted to 300 ethnic minority students per year to attend any U.S. college or university.

Questbridge Scholarship

$200,000 is granted to each of 1,464 students to be used over 4 years.

Hispanic Scholarship Fund

Approximately 10,000 winners - $30,000,000 awarded annually.

Thurgood Marshall College Fund

African Americans – approximately 500 scholarships per year (average award - $6,200 per year).

NAACP – National Association for the Advancement of Colored People

African Americans - about 170 students receive awards of $3,000 to $15,000.

Coca Cola Scholarship

1,400 students win scholarships (total amount awarded annually is approximately $3,550,000).

150 students receive $20,000 scholarship each.

NASSP – National Association of Secondary School Principals

600 NHS Scholarships awarded per year, 1 national winner ($25,000 scholarship). 24 national finalists ($5,625 each), 575 national semifinalists ($3,200 each). Apply between October 1 and December 1.

GE-Reagan Foundation Scholarship Program

$40,000 (10 students)

Another $50,000 is awarded in the Great Communicator Debate Series.

Scholastic Art and Writing Competition

Herblock Award - $1,000 scholarships for editorial cartoons

New York Life Award - $1,000 writing award about personal grief and loss

One Earth Award - $1,000 scholarship for writing about human-caused climate change

Portfolio Scholarships – Up to $10,000 granted for top portfolios

Civic Expression Award - $1,000 scholarships for writing on political and social issues

Best-In-Grade – Juror favorite awards receive $500 scholarships

College Tuition & Summer Scholarships - https://www.artandwriting.org/scholarships/

Gloria Barron Prize for Young Heroes

25 students each year ages 8 – 18 receive $10,000 for community service projects.

Prudential Spirit of Community Award (Prudential Emerging Visionaries)

25 students in grades 5 to 12 are granted a $1,000 - $5,000 award for community service.

Comcast NBCUniversal Leaders and Achievers Scholarship

More than 800 high school student winners each year win a $2,500 scholarship.

Brower Youth Awards

Environmental activism awards are granted to 6 winners; each receives $3,000.

Target Scholarship

HBCU Design Challenge for African Americans – Students submit designs for Black History Month.

Target Scholars Program – 1,000 students get $5,000 each.

Service/Leadership/Focused Organization Scholarship

Lions Club, Moose Club, Elks Club, Rotary Club, Soroptimists Club, Mensa

Parent Employment

Many companies offer scholarships for their employees and their children.

K-12 Educator Scholarship

This scholarship is for children with parents who teach in the K-12 system.

Distinguished Scholars Awards, Art Contest Scholarships

There are numerous scholarships that fall into these categories.

ROTC

These military scholarships are not given to everyone in ROTC.

A select group of outstanding candidates is given tuition, fees, textbooks, plus a monthly stipend.

PRESIDENT'S VOLUNTEER SERVICE AWARD

There is no money for this award, but it is nonetheless important to share. Individuals submit their community service hours and win these awards.

Hours Required to Earn Awards in Each Age Group

Age Group	Bronze	Silver	Gold	Lifetime Achievement Award
Kids (5–10 years old)	26–49 hours	50–74 hours	75+ hours	4,000+ hours
Teens (11–15)	50–74 hours	75–99 hours	100+ hours	4,000+ hours
Young Adults (16–25)	100–174 hours	175–249 hours	250+ hours	4,000+ hours
Adults (26+)	100–249 hours	250–499 hours	500+ hours	4,000+ hours

COLLEGE ADMISSIONS:

Success in the Face of Uncertainty

There are no guarantees in college admissions. However, planning is essential for success. The most beneficial advice is to pursue your passions with gusto, train to be the best you can be, take advantage of internships and experiences, and meet lots of people along the way.

Remember, "life is a journey, not a destination." Often the journey is more exciting, leading to lessons, friendships, and unforgettable moments. However, the fact is, in the end, if college is your goal, then you need to know a few action items to remember for success.

Should you worry about grades? Of course. You should also take classes that will challenge you. Colleges pick the best candidates from those who apply. Students must be academically prepared, socially conscious, and talented in a few different areas in which they are passionate (design, graphic arts, musical instruments, theatre, debate, public speaking, leadership, athletics, community service, computer coding, robotics, construction, etc.).

The college selection process is not that much different than companies picking employees. While colleges are more or less competitive, companies may have only one job, and a hundred resumes. Discover the unique drive and internal motivations within you that make you the very best you can be. Be exceptional at what you choose to do academically, personally, and professionally.

Most of all, You Do You

TALENT FOCUSED

Not all schools require high grades and test scores. Many are simply interested in selecting students who are the most talented, most driven, and the most willing to be team players on the college campus. Thus, while you should take a solid set of courses and fulfill the standard requirements, only the top schools emphasize completing a challenging curriculum while earning high grades and exemplary standardized test scores.

FOR HIGHLY SELECTIVE COLLEGES, TALENT IS JUST THE BEGINNING

A few highly selective colleges seek extraordinary talent over academics, but most zero in on a student's challenging courses and high grades. To gain admission into the most highly selective academic colleges, you must take the most challenging course load you can manage and succeed. Highly selective colleges want disciplined scholars AND remarkably talented students.

Determine what you can handle, knowing that some colleges with extremely competitive admissions standards will only take students who have completed more than ten AP, IB, or honors classes over the four years.

Why would the most competitive colleges require classes like AP Calculus or Physics for an art program? However daunting these classes may seem, remember, the top colleges have lots of applicants, and they need to draw the line somewhere. UCLA had 149,779 applicants for fall 2022; UC Berkeley had 128,192 applicants. The numbers are truly staggering since neither first-year class will have more than 7,000 students starting in the fall.

College admissions can feel like a rollercoaster of energy and emotion. Creating a portfolio of talent, training, and experience is just the beginning. Meanwhile, some colleges want to see standardized test scores aided by practice. Applications and essays may seem easy at first, but managing the various requirements and deadlines can be difficult. Therefore, this moment is a good time to get a calendar and organize your tasks.

REQUEST INFORMATION

Almost every college has a location, a link, or a 'contact us' page where you can request information from the school. If you are considering a school, request information from them. In this way, they may send you updates, scholarship opportunities, a valuable application fee waiver, special invites, and other information that could be valuable in the process. Of course, you may not need one more e-mail, and you may be receiving e-mails from the school anyway. Still, I recommend that you fill out their form. Then, since you are likely to be inundated with e-mails, make a file folder in your e-mail for all colleges you are considering. Then, when you get an e-mail from one of those schools, file it away.

STANDARDIZED TESTING

A few schools still require standardized testing. Check first. However, many colleges are 'test-optional'. This means that you are not required to take the SAT or ACT. However, if you have a good score, it may make all the difference in gaining admission. College admissions offices are studying this topic and considering their future policies. Much of their concern began with test cancelations worldwide due to the pandemic.

Schools did not want to let students into their site to take the test who may be infected, nor were they able to ensure safety. In addition, social distancing requirements limited the number of students who could take a test at any given site. Yet, for decades, college admissions decisions centered around grades and test scores. This change in the landscape of decision-making has rattled admissions departments.

Meanwhile, some colleges, proclaiming that they are 'test-optional', continue to leave a place to submit a score. Statistical evidence thus far shows that students who submit good scores are being accepted at a higher rate than those with similar grades and no score.

Colleges that are 'test blind' say they do not consider your scores. A few of these colleges still provide a place to input your scores. Thus, they are not truly

blind. Nevertheless, the decision regarding whether you take the test or submit the score is yours. If the school does not require an admissions test, you can choose to take the test and submit it as you like. If your academics are solid and you are willing to prepare for the test, you should take the test. If you do not think you will score well and the colleges you are considering do not require the test, focus on your portfolio.

APPLYING EARLY
Early Action (EA), Restricted Early Action (REA), and Early Decision (ED)

With low acceptance rates, the chance to get more scholarship money, and chaos surrounding the cancellations and changes in AP, IB, SAT, and ACT testing, students clamor to apply early to schools. In addition, applications to the top schools increased during the pandemic, resulting in colleges needing to make difficult admissions decisions in their quest to build a diverse, talented, and engaged class of students. Furthermore, students applying early have access to many more scholarship options. This confluence sent students in droves to apply early. This trend is likely to continue.

In Early Action (EA), Restricted Early Action (REA), and Early Decision (ED), students apply in late summer or early fall to college and generally find out around winter break, though some decisions come out earlier and a few arrive later. This advantage not only gives students a chance for more scholarship money in some cases but the benefit of finding out early reduces the tension of the long waiting period to find out about Regular Decision schools.

Early Action (EA) and Restricted Early Action (REA) are different. In restricted early action, a limitation is placed on either how many or what colleges you can apply to simultaneously. Many REA schools do not allow students to apply to other early action schools, though some will allow students to apply early to public colleges. Check the colleges to be sure. In addition, some schools like Georgetown will allow students to apply EA elsewhere but not apply to a binding Early Decision (ED) program where the student commits to attending if they are accepted. However, most EA schools do not have these restrictions, and some students apply to a handful of EA schools during the admissions process.

Early Decision (ED) is a binding agreement between the student and college with signatures from the student's parents and the high school assuring that the student is committed and will attend. Each of these parties acknowledges and agrees that, if granted admission, they will fulfill their agreement. There are caveats to this, though you should go into the agreement fully committing to your ED school.

There are incentives to applying ED. Frequently, acceptance rates are higher. Also, at some schools, a large percentage of their class is filled with students who profess their unequivocal love for their dream school. Students who know they have a top choice school, have the necessary admissions prerequisites fulfilled, and are committed to accepting the binding agreement to attend, should apply ED.

COMMON APPLICATION, COALITION APPLICATION, OR COLLEGE-SPECIFIC APPLICATION

Every college's process is unique. However, there are a few commonalities. In 2022, approximately 900 colleges used the Common App; about 150 colleges used the Coalition Application. A few used both. The University of California system has its own application as do the California State Universities and the Texas schools.

The Common App and Coalition App may be started early. In your junior year, consider getting a head start on reviewing what is required. The college-specific questions may change each year. However, the basic application is generally the same and can be created ahead of time. At the end of July, make a copy of everything you have completed just in case.

Some schools admit on a rolling basis. 'Rolling' means that periodically, after all of the materials are received, the admissions committee determines who they will accept, and they send the notification right away. Some students are accepted as early as August. The thrill of acceptance cannot be overstated.

ESSAYS

The Common Application and Coalition essays are often posted months ahead of time. Since this main essay is required or recommended for nearly all Common Application and Coalition Application schools, this is an excellent place to start thinking about what you might want to say to colleges.

In addition to the main essay on the Common Application and Coalition Application, about three-fours of the colleges have their own specific questions or essays. In August, most admissions applications are open and ready for you to dive into the college-specific questions, though many of the essay topics are available earlier, and some schools hold out until later for their big essay reveal.

These can be prepared ahead of time too. One popular question is, "What activity is most important to you and why?" Another is "Why did you choose your major?" A third common question is, "Why do you want to attend our school?" Others you should prepare or at least consider the topics of diversity, adversity, and challenges since these topics have become increasingly important in the admissions process. Everyone has a challenge they needed to overcome. What did you learn from that experience?

Complete the application fully. Think carefully about optional sections. Typically, universities offer you the chance to provide the school with just the right cherry on top of the ice cream sundae, allowing you to share something unique about you. If you have absolutely nothing to say, then leave it blank. There is an additional information section on the main Common App, Coalition Application, and University of California application. This location is not a place to write another essay, but you can include information that could not be adequately explained in the rest of the application.

There are also some schools that include scholarship essays within the supplement part of the application. Start early.

LETTERS OF RECOMMENDATION

Most colleges, though not all, request letters of recommendation from a counselor and one or more teachers. The university may want academic teachers and art teachers for drawing and painting programs. Plan for this. Occasionally, there is a section for optional recommendations too. In this location, you might get a recommendation from a summer program leader or someone with whom you did an internship. If you were in a sport, there is a location for a coach on about a quarter of the applications. Finally, if there is a supplemental application, for example, on SlideRoom, these often require separate recommendations reviewed by the art program.

DECISIONS, DECISIONS: WAITING FOR A RESPONSE

The period between submitting your application and getting your admissions results may not require a tremendous amount of work, but it does require patience and diligence. First, most schools will send you a link to a portal where you will check your results, though the most important reason for checking every couple of weeks is to ensure that the college is not missing something or has not offered you the chance to apply for an extra scholarship.

Check your portal regularly. Otherwise, read the college's correspondence sent through your e-mail. Waiting is difficult. These few months are a tough period because students want to know. However, the college typically lists the date they will send out the results on the portal. Other popular sites post their decision notification dates too. You will find out soon.

CELEBRATING ACCEPTANCES AND DEALING WITH REJECTION

Acceptance is not guaranteed. The probabilities are low at the most highly selective schools. However, you just need to work hard in school to have what it takes and give this commitment to academics all you have. When you find out the results, you will celebrate your acceptances.

Congratulations! The colleges in which you gain admission go on your list of wins. Check your financial aid and scholarship packages too. Money is often an important factor in making your decision. Consider visiting the school. Many students apply to college merely by someone's recommendation, *U.S. News and World Report* ranking, looking at campus photos on Google, or researching profiles posted on a website or in a book.

There is nothing that replaces the actual campus visit. After all, you will be spending a few years there. While you may not be accepted everywhere you apply, you may decide when you visit that the college is high on your list or that you do

not want to apply after all. Understandably, the pandemic's uncertainty added more question marks to an already complicated set of admissions processes.

The buzzword for 2020-2030 is resilience. It is never easy to be rejected. However, rejection happens, and you will survive this. Note that many colleges still accept applications in April, May, and June long after most school's applications are closed. Look up those colleges if you did not get accepted or if you want to see what other schools might be good options for you. In April and May, Google "College Openings Update". You will be surprised to see the colleges that show up on the list that still have open spots.

WAITLISTS: THE ART OF WAITING

Immediately confirm if you are given a waitlist spot and still want to attend. There is often a deadline. You do not want to miss this. If you are no longer interested or have selected another school, go into the portal and turn down the offer. Someone else is bound to be thrilled by your anonymous gift.

If you are still interested, find the location on the portal or site designated by the college to update them on what you have done – accomplishments, awards, extra class, honors, art, shows, or films. You only want to add what they have not yet seen, but if you have taken the initiative to do something more than what you originally stated on the application, by all means, tell them.

You could just wait for their decision, but you are better off being proactive and showing that you really want to be at their school. Students do get off the waitlists at most schools. How much do you want to attend? Meanwhile, you will have to deposit somewhere else before the May 1st deadline. Stay hopeful. This next year will be a significant step along your journey. Relax!

CHAPTER 8

SUPPLEMENTAL MATERIALS AND PORTFOLIOS FOR DRAWING & PAINTING PROGRAMS

"A work of art which did not begin in emotion is not art."

– Paul Cézanne

At the top art and design schools like Rhode Island School of Design, School of Visual Arts, New York University, CalArts, Parsons School of Design, School of the Art Institute of Chicago, and Washington University in St. Louis, acceptance is very difficult. Furthermore, the BFA degree is completely immersive. Inspired by the environment, you will be surrounded by students who are creative, multitalented, and focused.

Students must be wholly dedicated to art. Thus, admissions officers and art school directors are keenly interested in the applicant's talent and commitment. As a result, a portfolio review is required for the top schools; sometimes, an interview is part of the admissions process as well. Applicants must demonstrate ability and potential.

CHANGES IN THE APPLICANT DEMOGRAPHICS
CHALLENGES ON THE ROAD AHEAD

COVID-19 shook students as well as admissions offices. Many studio-centered programs closed down or went online. International students left for their country of origin and classes at a distance could not provide the needed materials, space, and opportunities. Many quit and did not return.

Furthermore, some art programs completely shut down. Colleges faced a crisis. While some programs reopened after COVID-19 and some students returned, demographic shifts resulted, including gender diversity and ethnic makeup.

Additionally, the decreased population of international students shook art programs. Nevertheless, many students still applied.

Other challenges existed as well. COVID-19 changed the makeup of applicants to college. Many students of color chose not to apply. Other data show that while enrollments rebounded, some programs suffered from budget cuts.

NATIONAL PORTFOLIO DAYS

These online and in-person national events are free for students to participate anywhere they are located in the world. In-person events are often held both inside and outside of the United States. Prospective art program applicants have the chance to meet admissions staff and present art pieces. Students must register online. There are filters with the online registration so you can sign up for events that fit your needs: online in-person, undergraduates, transfer, or graduate school.

In-person events can be jam-packed with people, though COVID-19 changed procedures with limited numbers of individuals inside venues. In the past, massive lines where students waited for their turn sometimes resulted in disappointed latecomers. In some locations, now, there is a reservation system. Make sure you read about any required protocols for in-person events.

More than fifty colleges come to many of the in-person events. Typically, you will have 10 to 15 minutes to speak to a representative and show them your work. You should bring a range of pieces. The website recommends bringing 10 – 12 pieces. Even if you only bring five, you are fine. The point is for your work to be reviewed so you can gain valuable feedback and improve.

For the online events, there are live sessions where you wait in a 'waiting room' queue until you can be seen. You can also schedule a meeting, though only on the day of the event. You may register for multiple school reviews. Note that you will not upload your portfolio. Rather, you will meet with your reviewer via Zoom and share your screen.

These events do not guarantee admission, and no admissions decisions are made at these events. In addition, although the colleges may suggest that you apply for their scholarships or be considered for their merit awards, you will not be awarded any money at these events.

In most cases, you will still need to present your portfolio online through the school-determined application portal. Even so, these events are excellent in that they allow you to meet people from various colleges and they get a chance to meet you. Furthermore, you get helpful advice and suggestions on how you can improve the pieces you plan to submit.

ART SCHOOL ADMISSIONS

RISD offers its own portfolio days online, where they will review your work and give you a valuable critique. Hint: RISD looks for engaged learners who will connect with the world. They want art that says something meaningful, evokes emotion and shares a point of view. Being technically strong is essential, but being emotionally strong and inextricably linked to the audience is imperative. Thus, more is not better. Only share your best work.

Portfolios are required at many art colleges. Since students often apply to 10-20 schools, the effort can be daunting. Furthermore, completing applications and creating portfolios take time and money for training, preparation, application fees, and other expenses. For some schools, there are fee waivers.

PORTFOLIO REQUIREMENTS

The first entry point to art programs is investigating colleges. Apply to your dream school, but also select colleges that have programs that fit your criteria – classes, program requirements, geography, studio space, faculty, career prospects, cost, etc. For now, let's look at the portfolio requirements at a few schools. Start by getting a general idea of what each school requires so that you are prepared. More information is provided in the profiles later on in this book.

CALIFORNIA INSTITUTE OF THE ARTS

4-year BFA in Art

Students must complete the online application, fees, artist statement, two letters of recommendation, and transcripts. In the CalArts portfolio section, include 15-20 images of any medium. A variety of types of work is preferred. Sketches or works in progress are acceptable. Do not use a pre-formatted portfolio as images must be individual, not composited, PDFs, or website links. Make sure the image fills the slide. Provide captions, descriptions, and titles in the "edit details" area. Do not include generic work like technical exercises, figure/life drawings, or still life drawings. You will also submit a 30-90 second video introduction.

NEW YORK UNIVERSITY

BFA Studio Art

After completing the Common Application, students will submit an "Artistic Review" from your application status page. Media uploads can include images of artwork (drawing, painting, sculpture, video, photography, digital art, etc.) that represent your artistic interests while also demonstrating your technical abilities and imagination. You must include 12-15 images of recent artwork in any medium. You will also present a one-page "Statement of Purpose".

PARSONS SCHOOL OF ART AND DESIGN

BFA Fine Arts; BFA Communication Design

Parsons requests an uploaded portfolio of eight to twelve images from a student's breadth of media skills, including drawing, painting, sculpture, design, collage, animation, etc. Experimentation, imagination, and self-expression are key. Include documentation and descriptions of your work and process. Parsons also requires a submission called "The Parsons Challenge". Start this part early. Many students put this off, and either do a lackluster job or cannot pull this together before the deadline. The Parsons Challenge is a new visual work inspired by a theme expressed in work within the portfolio. Students submit a required 500-word essay describing the development of the idea. Two additional pieces may be added to document your process. Observational work is not required since technique and vision are emphasized in the review.

RHODE ISLAND SCHOOL OF DESIGN

BFA Painting
Concentration Option in Drawing

After completing the Common Application, students will submit a SlideRoom supplement. Students present 12-20 examples of their recent artwork on the SlideRoom site. RISD requests finished pieces, drawings from direct observation, and no more than three pieces that show research and prep work. RISD's admissions are competitive, so you should curate and edit the pieces you choose to submit in your portfolio.

SCHOOL OF THE ART INSTITUTE OF CHICAGO

BFA Painting & Drawing
BFA Art & Technology Studies
BFA Visual Communication Design

Submit the Common Application, noting the merit scholarship deadlines and specific requirements. All programs require a SlideRoom portfolio. Develop the 250-500-word artist's statement describing how and why you created the pieces you submitted and how your experiences contributed to your thinking. Include 10-15 creative works that demonstrate your potential from observational to abstract.

All media are considered, though SAIC suggests submitting those that are bold, inventive, thought-provoking, expressive, and risk-taking. You may concentrate on a single media or any combination of drawings, prints, photographs, paintings, film, video, audio recordings, sculpture, ceramics, fashion designs, graphic design, furniture, objects, architectural designs, websites, video games, sketchbooks, scripts, storyboards, screenplays, and zines.

SCHOOL OF VISUAL ARTS

BFA Fine Arts
Concentrations: Painting, Drawing, Printmaking, Sculpture, & Installation

Apply through the SVA site and submit a portfolio of 15-20 images of your strongest artwork through SlideRoom. Include samples of your drawing with a minimum of 3-5 examples from direct observation (self-portraits, figure drawings, object studies, still life, and landscape). Other media, like painting, photography, printmaking, collage, etc., are welcome. Sketchbooks, shown at in-person reviews, offer valuable insights. Do not focus on computer-generated images.

WASHINGTON UNIVERSITY IN ST. LOUIS

BFA Art
Concentrations in Painting, Photography, Printmaking,
Sculpture, Time-Based + Media Art
BA Art; BA Design

After completing the Common Application, College of Art students will submit a SlideRoom supplement. All art applicants are considered for the Conway or Poretz Scholarship in art. Media uploads of 12 – 15 images can include recent work drawings, 2-D pieces, 3-D models, photography, video, etc.

CHAPTER 9

POST PANDEMIC EMPLOYMENT OUTLOOK: STATISTICS AND ECONOMIC PROJECTIONS

"I never paint dreams or nightmares. I paint my own reality."

– Frida Kahlo

84

rtists often enter many different fields and play essential roles in society. According to the *Occupational Outlook Handbook*, employment opportunities in these fields are slated to grow from 2020 to 2030 at different rates with new jobs expected. The median annual wage for entry-level positions is given below. The job outlook for artists is good with a 14% growth rate. Wages are also likely to increase.

According to the 2022 Bureau of Labor Statistics,[1]

OCCUPATION	JOB SUMMARY	ENTRY-LEVEL EDUCATION	MEDIAN PAY
Advertising Sales and Agents	Advertising sales agents sell advertising space to businesses and individuals.	High School Diploma or Equivalent	$52,340
Archivists, Curators, and Museum Workers	Archivists and curators oversee institutions' collections, such as historical items or of artwork. Museum technicians and conservators prepare and restore items in those collections.	Varies	$50,120
Art Directors	Art directors are responsible for the visual style and images in magazines, newspapers, product packaging, and movie and television productions.	Bachelor's Degree	$100,890
Broadcast, Sound, and Video Technicians	Broadcast, sound, and video technicians set up, operate, and maintain electrical equipment for media programs.	Varies	$49,050
Craft and Fine Artists	Craft and fine artists use a variety of materials and techniques to create art for sale and exhibition.	Varies	$49,960
Dancers and Choreographers	Dancers and choreographers use dance performances to express ideas and stories.	Varies	N/A
Desktop Publishers	Desktop publishers use computer software to design page layouts for items that are printed or published online.	Associate's Degree	$46,910

1   Bureau of Labor Statistics, U.S. Department of Labor, *Occupational Outlook Handbook*, Craft and Fine Artists, at https://www.bls.gov/ooh/arts-and-design/craft-and-fine-artists.htm.

OCCUPATION	JOB SUMMARY	ENTRY-LEVEL EDUCATION	MEDIAN PAY
Editors	Editors plan, review, and revise content for publication.	Bachelor's Degree	$63,350
Fashion Designers	Fashion designers create clothing, accessories, and footwear.	Bachelor's Degree	$77,450
Film and Video Editors & Camera Operators	Film and video editors and camera operators manipulate moving images that entertain or inform an audience.	Bachelor's Degree	$60,360
Graphic Designers	Graphic designers create visual concepts, using computer software or by hand, to communicate ideas that inspire, inform, and captivate consumers.	Bachelor's Degree	$50,710
Industrial Designers	Industrial designers combine art, business, and engineering to develop the concepts for manufactured products.	Bachelor's Degree	$77,030
Jewelers & Precious Stone & Metal Workers	Jewelers and precious stone and metal workers design, construct, adjust, repair, appraise and sell jewelry.	Bachelor's Degree	$46,640
Market Research Analysts	Market research analysts study market conditions to examine potential sales of a product or service.	Bachelor's Degree	$63,920
News Analysts, Reporters, and Journalists	News analysts, reporters, and journalists keep the public updated about current events and noteworthy information.	Bachelor's Degree	$48,370
Postsecondary Teachers	Postsecondary teachers instruct students in a variety of academic subjects beyond the high school level.	Master's Degree	$79,640
Producers and Directors	Producers and directors make business and creative decisions about film, television, stage, and other productions.	Bachelor's Degree	$79,000

OCCUPATION	JOB SUMMARY	ENTRY-LEVEL EDUCATION	MEDIAN PAY
Public Relations & Fundraising Managers	Public relations managers direct the creation of materials that will enhance the public image of their employer or client. Fundraising managers coordinate campaigns that bring in donations for their organization.	Bachelor's Degree	$119,860
Public Relations Specialists	Public relations specialists create and maintain a positive public image for the clients they represent.	Bachelor's Degree	$62,800
Sales Managers	Sales managers direct organizations' sales teams.	Bachelor's Degree	$127,490
Photographers	Photographers use their technical expertise, creativity, and composition skills to produce and preserve images.	Bachelor's Degree	$38,950
Special Effects Artists & Animators	Special effects artists and animators create images that appear to move and visual effects for various forms of media and entertainment.	Bachelor's Degree	$78,790
Technical Writers	Technical writers prepare instruction manuals, how-to guides, journal articles, and other supporting documents to communicate complex and technical information more easily.	Bachelor's Degree	$78,060
Woodworkers	Woodworkers manufacture a variety of products, such as cabinets and furniture, using wood, veneers, and laminates.	High School Diploma or Equivalent	$36,710
Writers and Authors	Writers and authors develop written content for various types of media.	Bachelor's Degree	$67,120

We know what we are but know not what we may be.

– William Shakespeare

Artists work in studios where they immortalize ideas in a job that is a cross between artist, Imagineer, and digital content expert. The median pay for an artist is $49,120 for those with a bachelor's degree. Those with a master's degree are typically paid higher due to their more specialized, focused knowledge. The employment prospects for artists are positive with 7,000 new jobs expected in 2022.

Similar jobs, listed in the previous chart, vary across subjects since artists have different focuses. The fluidity and opportunity in art across travel, nature, marketing, journalism, and fashion run the gamut of options, not to mention portrait work. Society has a wide and varied use for the skills of an artist. However, you will need to discover your personal areas of interest.

The skills an art student learns in school, including drawing, painting, graphic design, printmaking, package design, illustration, comic book art, collage, sculpture, ceramics, crafts, and computer-aided design are valuable and transferrable to other fields as well. According to the Bureau of Labor Statistics, approximately 54% of artists are self-employed while 7% work in the federal government, 7% in independent jobs, 5% in the motion picture and sound recording industries, and 3% work in personal care services.[2]

IMPACT OF COVID-19

COVID-19 impacted the number of jobs people could get in art. A significant drop in opportunities led most artists to the internet to post their art and set up their independent work for freelancing. The dynamic changed as Pinterest, Instagram, and Facebook became inundated with images. One of my friends in the publishing business said that freelancers needed a "megaphone" or "gimmick" to get noticed. He is not a gimmicky kind of guy, so he searches for platforms to broadcast his work. Thus, the impact of COVID-19 cannot be understated. While the field is booming with more entrants presenting what they created, practicing continues to be essential, and technique can always be improved.

ROAD TO BECOMING AN ARTIST

The road to success in this industry should not be discouraging since a few steps are required along the way. Even so, achieving the goal is rewarding. Encourage those around you. If this is the field you want to pursue, pave the road in front of you and drive.

---

2 Bureau of Labor Statistics, U.S. Department of Labor, *Occupational Outlook Handbook*, Craft and Fine Artists, at https://www.bls.gov/ooh/arts-and-design/craft-and-fine-artists.htm

An internship or apprenticeship or two in peripheral areas would not hurt you in your pursuit of gigs and contract work. Although some internships are unpaid, you will find that most applicants will have one or more. Some internships pay fairly well. Even if you will ultimately be a freelancer, you might find parallel bread and butter professions while you fine-tune your craft.

If you are serious, you will make a fantastic career out of your pursuit. Initiative-taking persistence, talent, creativity, and moxie can get you into your desired college program and career. You may have to start at the very bottom of the ladder, but you can climb the rungs methodically one by one.

Companies want to know employees' work ethic, personality, and professionalism. An internship allows you to get to know the corporate climate better and allows others to get to know you better too. Thus, many companies hire the interns they feel are the best fit rather than choosing candidates from the piles of resumes that have been submitted.

Education unlocks doors no matter which direction your career takes you. Whatever direction you pursue, if you lay a foundation, undaunted by the competition, and are unafraid of starting at the bottom, you will do fine. Hard work and creativity go a long way in this industry. Start by getting a solid education.

MANAGEMENT AND EMPLOYEE RETENTION

Skills to Know: Management, Human Resources, Social Consciousness, Ethics

One of the most significant challenges facing employers in the years from 2022 - 2030 will be locating and retaining talent. The pandemic slowed education and learning with online classes, reduced access to faculty/advising, limited access to labs, inability to attend workshops, retail closures, and fewer conferences, meetings, and shows. Health concerns rose to the top of importance as did financial stress, job uncertainty, and social consciousness.

Many students chose to work rather than study and start online stores when they could not access locations for community service or continue with their sport, instrument, or hobbies. With the changes in lifestyle and fears about health, safety, and wellness, many bright and talented students developed a fearless sense of autonomy and independence, while for others, the necessary skills ordinarily developed in school were fraught by limitations.

Finding talent within the changing hiring atmosphere will require new skills to retain staff. Employees are increasingly looking elsewhere for a better opportunity. This development will require managers to earn and harness employee trust and loyalty.

The digital workforce has also placed demands on human resources. While many companies want their employees to work in-person, the convenience of working at home and the drudgery of commuting to work have created an environment where employees seek greater flexibility. Changes are coming. The employee talent challenge is likely to create a more global workforce where companies look for less expensive online talent from a pool of eager workers in other countries.

CHAPTER 10

NEXT STEPS: PREPARATION AND REAL-WORLD SKILLS

"An artist is not paid for his labor but for his vision."

– James McNeill Whistler

C ollege offers you the freedom to express yourself openly, dynamically, and interactively. As you explore art in society, you will explore the art within you, hungering to emerge. The next step for you is to choose a college where your persona fits into the makeup of the environment. In college studios, you will receive personalized, interactive training, immersed and infused with inspiration from fellow classmates.

Each drawing or painting you produce will leave a lasting impression. Through social media, instantaneously, you can share your art with millions of people in a matter of moments. The possibilities are limitless. In school or out of school, you may want to take a few classes on social media dynamics and website editing. Furthermore, on the leading edge of the Metaverse, you can create opportunities that were never before possible. It's unbelievably thrilling.

Art is a dynamic, multidimensional world where you contribute to the dialogue. In some careers, repetitive tasks and uninspiring projects lead employees to loathe their jobs and tick off minutes until their day is done. Yet, your life will undoubtedly be different and ever-changing since the world around you will change from moment to moment. Over time, whichever area of art becomes your focus, you will earn your way to a career of endless possibilities.

American landscape painter, George Inness, shared, "The true use of art is, first, to cultivate the artist's own spiritual nature." Spend time thinking, even though time sometimes seems short. You may feel as if time slips through your fingers like sand in an hourglass. Resist the temptation to upload your art before contemplating what you want to express. While social media opens doors to share your artwork, truly magical works are created when time stands still, and you immerse yourself in a creative state.

Today is a precious moment. As you contemplate college choices and tomorrow's future, you will explore your passion, open doors you never expected, and discover opportunities that will tantalize and challenge you along the way. As such, you will capture a new, exciting, and eclectic way of life.

Attending a respected school can help you get noticed. Your next steps are aided by connections offered by professors, classmates, and alumni. Networking at events is also an excellent way to discover opportunities. Shows, displays, and contests in school, out of school, in the summer, or through social media can help you get noticed. Bring people into your world, allowing them to feel and interpret art in their unique way.

Throughout your varied experiences, you will meet other artists who may recommend you or inform you about open positions or contract opportunities, even some that are not publicly announced. In addition, many schools have a culminating event where you can put your best foot forward and showcase your work. Exposure to industry professionals can open new doors while interacting with people online or in-person will allow you to maintain those connections.

Autonomy and freedom to choose the jobs you take by venturing out on your own may seem alluring, but freelancing may result in uncertainty or even career limitations. As a result, companies often choose seasoned professionals with work experience in other firms. However, there are ways to mitigate against the lean times of solo work. A few options include demonstrating mastery, producing amazing work, resolving client problems, aligning ideologies, and initially charging less. Despite challenges, put yourself out there.

You could wait for the phone to ring to be discovered. However, you should post regularly and be out and about for that to happen. Some individuals pine away, hoping to be selected and deciding which organization would be a perfect fit. Others decide that they only want to work at a specific firm or location. Still others determine that they will work for themselves and be their own boss. Yet, sometimes taking any position at the start is a steppingstone to your dream life, commitment to service, and opportunity to put your unique mark on society.

BOLD NETWORKING

Networking takes social skills and a bit of moxie. From elevator speeches and professional encounters to interviews and masterclasses, your job is to find a way to get your work in front of people and have them see your talent and your potential to contribute. You have something special and fresh ideas. Finally, there is a professional entity that will welcome your style, ingenuity, discipline, and impact.

How can you be recognized? Meet people; hand out your resume; give them your business card; ask for their business card; follow up; ask if you can call or meet them, even when approaching these professionals may seem uncomfortable. Stay in touch with people you meet, even if it is just happenstance or serendipity. Keep a log with each person's phone, e-mail, identifying information, and both date and location where you met. You never know when you will need it.

If you meet people professionally at a masterclass or workshop, even if you do not exchange information, you will recognize them at a later date. They may recognize you in a future event too. Keep training. You should always seek ways to improve, irrespective of your experience. Lifelong learning improves your ability to maintain up-to-date skills and transition to new ventures. The outside world's perspective changes more quickly with social media's instant influences.

Though you should not take workshops just for the sake of meeting people, when you attend, be present in your quest to lead, serve, and envision. If your focus is not on your improvement or development, you may appear insincere in your intentions. However, workshops, conferences, and contests can allow others to see your purpose, vision, and talent.

Big-ticket training does not always mean better trainers or opportunities. Find time to visit museums, survey your surroundings, and notice cultural changes. While gathering new thoughts, remember humility and open-mindedness go a long way. Defer to the wise and listen. There is much you can learn.

STAY IN TOUCH

Do not annoy busy people, but you can keep in touch every couple of months. Communicating more frequently is overwhelming. However, life is long. People who grow with their craft transition fluidly through life's career phases. In drawing and painting, contacts are essential in all phases of your career. Also, do not be surprised. Many go-getters seeking to gain a coveted contract do the following:

1. Speak at Chamber of Commerce meetings.
2. Attend art, design, and software trade shows.
3. Gain a following on Instagram and Pinterest.
4. Write a newsletter and publish it on LinkedIn and other sources.
5. Link your work to Facebook, Twitter, Instagram, Pinterest, and other social media.
6. Enter in art contests.
7. Join professional associations.
8. Attend social gatherings of potential customers.
9. Keep in touch with your professors.
10. Stay involved with your alumni associations.

Friendships matter. Become lifelong colleagues by finding friends who share mutual interests and offer a sounding board or connections to new opportunities. People tend to stay in touch with "important" people. Note to self: Your contemporaries or peers are important people...although possibly not yet. As you form lists of contacts, you are likely to know these people throughout your career.

Be audacious while also being authentic. Networking can sometimes appear fake or forced as if you are going out on a hunt to find people for your own benefit. Worse, the act of networking can appear like stalking for those who incessantly attempt to connect.

The mental image of this type of 'networking' conjures the vision of people congregating at meetings. Friendships and the mutual support of allies can be enormously helpful, though 20,000 or even 200,000 followers on your website do not mean you are popular. However, you can have unexpected meaningful exchanges if you get out, meet people, and live life.

There are times when deeply moving, casual conversations in non-professional settings could also turn into connections. Do not lose touch with people or burn bridges along the way. This industry is not that big, especially whatever subspecialty you choose. You will continually see extraordinary talent. You never know. They may contact you to collaborate one day or meet for coffee at an event.

COLLEGE AND CAREER CENTERS

Although art programs often have internal connections to help you secure an internship or job, you might also speak to someone at your campus career center. They often have interesting and possibly different prospects you might not get elsewhere. In addition, there may be a specific career liaison for their art programs. Connect with them for help in your search process. Besides, you might want a related job that utilizes your creative, design, problem-solving, and presentation skills.

Companies that attend comic book shows often hire graduates whose energy, initiative, and cutting-edge knowledge are invaluable. Design, camera, and software companies also appreciate those who can demonstrate their products. Adobe, for example, has more than 24,000 employees worldwide. These jobs may or may not be your dream job now, but you might be surprised where the position may lead you, and sometimes you just need employment to earn money and get yourself on your feet.

Career center coordinators often have excellent ideas of alternative options you may have never considered. Furthermore, they can assist you with creating a professional resume and cover letters for specific industries that are different from the ones you have for drawing and painting.

They may also connect you with past graduates in the industry who make excellent connections. Some of them may have been in your program and have been through the ropes, know a few people, and may be able to get you an interview or invite you to an industry event. Any contact may help you get your foot in the door or find a job to make money in the meantime.

LINKEDIN

LinkedIn is especially helpful for career searches. You can find numerous influential contacts on LinkedIn. After interviews or events, connect with each person you met on LinkedIn. Keep a contact list of individuals you get to know in your area of interest. Do not constantly try to connect with people you do not really know. However, if you have made the connection, occasionally keep in touch.

While some LinkedIn message boxes may be full and you may not get a reply, you can try. Some people have tens of thousands of LinkedIn followers. I have about 20,000 'contacts', which does not necessarily mean that I am important. Remember that a paycheck or lots of friends does not make you more worthy or successful. Worth and value emanate from within your heart. Occasionally, you hit on a lucky break. Though I do not have time to communicate with everyone, I have connected with some of my most inspiring authors, advisors, and intellectual leaders through LinkedIn.

FINALLY

Most people are willing to help you. Five percent will not. Thus, you have a 19 out of 20 chance of interacting with decent people who have the time and will give you advice. Don't lose faith in humanity just because you run into a few people who are too busy to stop for you or are too self-absorbed that they cannot answer your question.

Remember that talent is only the beginning. You need to sell yourself. As you organize your goals and responsibilities, remember to think one step ahead of where you want to be by making a game plan. Since actions speak louder than words, take action without complaining and spread kindness along the way. Burned bridges are tough to reconstruct.

Honesty and trustworthiness are worth more than any physical object. Earn this by working hard, being efficient, and telling the truth. Professionalism in your words and deeds is essential. Put away distractions and focus on tasks. Texts and social media take a surprising amount of time. Every action you take is a steppingstone to your future. Discipline is achieved by creating a goal and making it happen.

A nice note, card, or gift reminds people you are thinking about them, even when you are incredibly busy. Good friends who have your best interest may know doors that are not yet open for you. Keep in touch with them.

So, go on a walk, meet people, and live fully. Serendipity happens when you live life. However, your education is immensely valuable. Success happens when preparation meets opportunity. Thus, preparation is the best way to generate luck. Finally, even the most disciplined person can be lazy or inefficient. Fight this. Stay active. Make your life happen for you. Here are a few things to remember as you go out to pursue your dreams.

- Work ethic is everything.
- Excellence is expected.
- Learn what you do not know on your own time.
- Come to work prepared.
- Take constructive criticism well.
- Be respectful and courteous.
- Keep your cool under pressure.
- Avoid being timid.
- Stay on task.
- Come early.
- Stay late.
- Take your work seriously.
- Do more than expected.
- Be humble and thoughtful.
- Read e-mail/texts after hours.
- Ask questions. No question is too stupid.
- The only stupid question is the one that is never asked.
- Maintain a clean workspace.
- Dress and act professionally.
- Don't gossip or complain.
- Play when you are done.
- Study hard, play hard – in that order.
- Avoid frustrating your phenomenally busy supervisor.
- Be straightforward, and don't beat around the bush.

You've Got This!

4
Regions

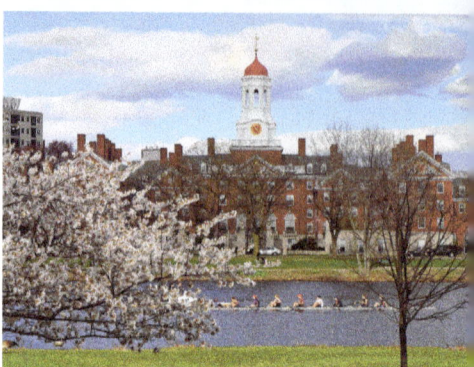

52
Programs

COLLEGE PROFILES AND REQUIREMENTS

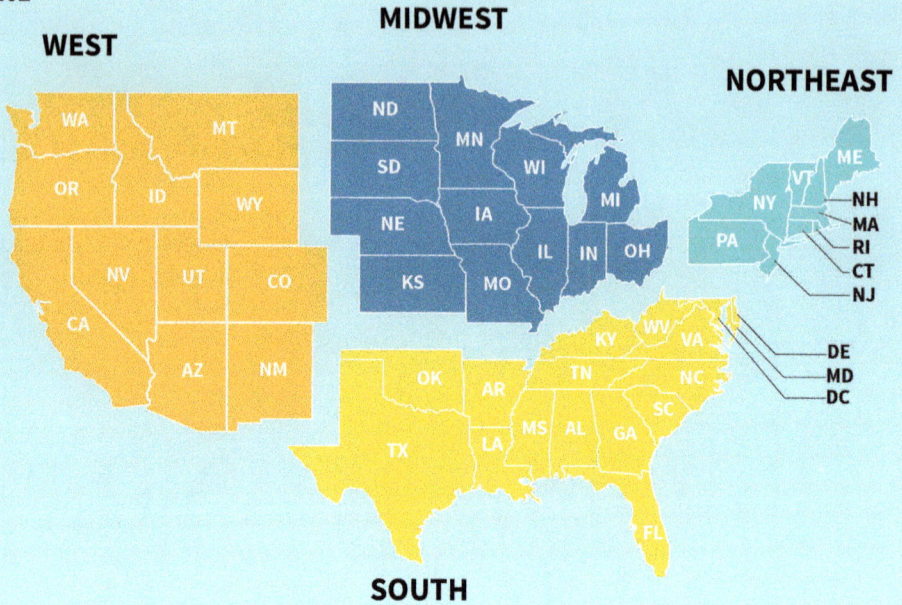

WEST

MIDWEST

NORTHEAST

SOUTH

PROGRAMS BY REGION
U.S. CENSUS BUREAU CLASSIFICATIONS

REGION 1 – NORTHEAST

Connecticut, Maine, Massachusetts, New Hampshire, New Jersey, New York, Pennsylvania, Rhode Island, and Vermont

REGION 2 – MIDWEST

Illinois, Indiana, Iowa, Kansas, Michigan, Minnesota, Missouri, Nebraska, North Dakota, Ohio, South Dakota, and Wisconsin

REGION 3 – SOUTH

Alabama, Arkansas, Delaware, District of Columbia, Florida, Georgia, Kentucky, Louisiana, Maryland, Mississippi, North Carolina, Oklahoma, South Carolina, Tennessee, Texas, Virginia, and West Virginia

REGION 4 – WEST

Alaska, Arizona, California, Colorado, Hawaii, Idaho, Montana, Nevada, New Mexico, Oregon, Utah, Washington, and Wyoming

LIST OF DRAWING & PAINTING PROGRAMS

The 52 programs listed in the following pages include profiles of the top undergraduate drawing and painting programs as of April 2022 along with additional college programs that offer closely related degrees. Many students interested in drawing and painting are often also interested in 3-D design, illustration, graphic art, animation, and film. Those schools are profiled in other books, though some lists are provided in the back.

Majoring in drawing and painting is not for everyone. Although immensely rewarding, success requires initiative. Some students dual major for greater flexibility. In college, students discover their priorities, commitments, and perseverance. A few choose an alternative path somewhere down the road.

Thus, this book provides you with lists for other areas of art programs so you can explore those options. Keep the book handy. Even after you begin college, you may find that the summer and alternative college programs are helpful.

Creating lists is often tedious and cumbersome. These lists were gathered to help you with this task.

Descriptions of the college programs, tuition, requirements, and deadlines are accurate as of April 2022. However, the requirements may have changed by the time you purchase this book. Nevertheless, this information is a great place to start!

Note: To simplify the text and fit information into the charts and descriptions, abbreviations were used as well as shortened sentences and acronyms.

CHAPTER 11

REGION ONE

NORTHEAST

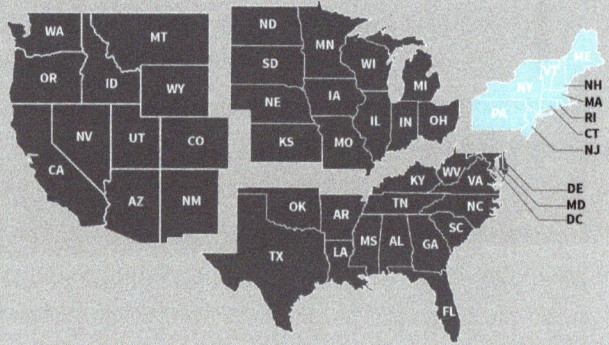

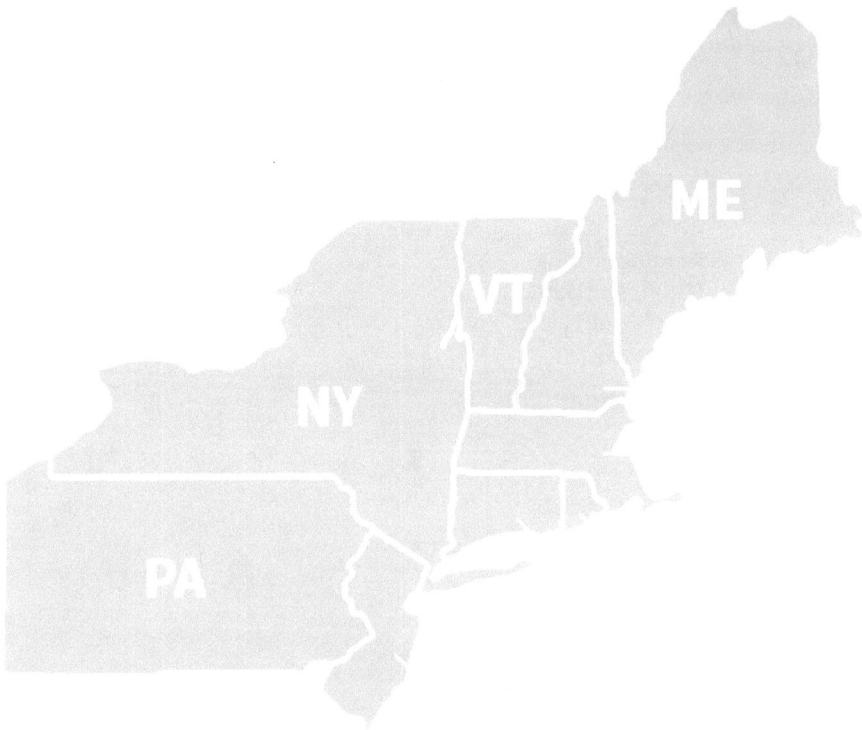

1. *CT - Yale University*
2. *MA - Boston University*
3. *MA - Massachusetts College of Art & Design*
4. *NJ - Rutgers, The State University of New Jersey*
5. *NY - Bard College*
6. *NY - Columbia University*
7. *NY - Cooper Union*
8. *NY - CUNY Hunter College*
9. *NY - Parsons School of Design*
10. *NY - Pratt Institute*
11. *NY - School of Visual Arts*
12. *NY - SUNY Buffalo*
13. *NY - Syracuse University*
14. *PA - Arcadia University*
15. *PA - Pennsylvania Academy of Fine Arts (PAFA)*
16. *PA - Temple University*
17. *RI - Providence College*
18. *RI - Rhode Island School of Design*

DRAWING & PAINTING PROGRAMS

School	Avg. GPA, SAT Evidence-Based Reading Writing (ERW), SAT Math (M), and ACT Composite (C) / Early Decision (ED): Yes/No	Admission Statistics	Program(s)	Portfolio Required (req.)
Yale University 220 York Street, Room 102, New Haven, CT 06511	GPA: N/A SAT (ERW): 720-780 SAT (M): 740-800 ACT (C): 33-35 ED: No, but Restrictive Early Action (REA) available	Overall College Admit Rate: 7% Undergrad Enrollment: 4,664 Total Enrollment: 12,060	BA Art, specialization: Painting/Printmaking	Portfolio optional
Boston University 233 Bay State Road, Boston, MA 02215	GPA: 3.76 SAT (ERW): 640-720 SAT (M): 670-780 ACT (C): 30-34 ED: Yes	Overall College Admit Rate: 20% Undergrad Enrollment: 16,872 Total Enrollment: 32,718	BFA Painting	Portfolio req.
Massachusetts College of Art & Design 621 Huntington Ave, Boston, MA 02115	GPA: N/A SAT (ERW): N/A SAT (M): N/A ACT (C): N/A *Test-optional ED: No	Admit Rate: 70% Undergrad Enrollment: 1,770 Total Enrollment: 1,894	BFA Painting	Portfolio req.
Rutgers, The State University of New Jersey 100 Sutphen Road, Piscataway, NJ 08854	GPA: N/A SAT (ERW): 580-680 SAT (M): 600-730 ACT (C): 25-32 ED: No	Overall College Admit Rate: 67% Undergrad Enrollment: 35,844 Total Enrollment: 50,411	BFA Visual Arts, concentrations: Drawing, Painting BA Art, concentration: Drawing	Portfolio req.

School	Avg. GPA, SAT Evidence-Based Reading Writing (ERW), SAT Math (M), and ACT Composite (C) Early Decision (ED): Yes/No	Admission Statistics	Program(s)	Portfolio Required (req.)
Bard College 30 Campus Road, Annandale-on-Hudson, NY 12504	GPA: N/A SAT (ERW): N/A* SAT (M): N/A* ACT (C): N/A* *Test-optional ED: Yes	Overall College Admit Rate: 57% Undergrad Enrollment: 2,118 Total Enrollment: 2,456	BA Studio Arts	Portfolio optional
Columbia University 1130 Amsterdam Avenue, New York, NY 10027	GPA: N/A SAT (ERW): 720-770 SAT (M): 740-800 ACT (C): 33-35 ED: Yes	Overall College Admit Rate: 4% Undergrad Enrollment: 8,448 Total Enrollment: 31,455	BA Visual Arts, concentration: Drawing, Painting	Portfolio optional
The Cooper Union 30 Cooper Sq, New York, NY 10003	GPA: 3.75 SAT (ERW): 650-740 SAT (M): 655-790 ACT (C): 30-35 ED: Yes	Overall College Admit Rate: 18% Undergrad Enrollment: 806 Total Enrollment: 887	BFA Art	Portfolio req.
CUNY Hunter College 695 Park Ave, New York, NY 10065	GPA: N/A SAT (ERW): 580-650 SAT (M): 590-690 ACT (C): 25-31 ED: No	Admit Rate: 40% Undergrad Enrollment: 17,943 Total Enrollment: 24,052	BFA Studio Art, concentrations: Drawing, Painting	Portfolio not req.

NORTHEAST

DRAWING & PAINTING PROGRAMS

School	Avg. GPA, SAT Evidence-Based Reading Writing (ERW), SAT Math (M), and ACT Composite (C) Early Decision (ED): Yes/No	Admission Statistics	Program(s)	Portfolio Required (req.)
Parsons - The New School 66 Fifth Avenue, New York, NY 10011	GPA: N/A SAT (ERW): 580-680 SAT (M): 560-680 ACT (C): 26-30 ED: No	Admit Rate: 69% Undergrad Enrollment: 6,399 Total Enrollment: 9,047	BFA Fine Arts	Portfolio req.
Pratt Institute 200 Willoughby Avenue, Brooklyn, NY 11205	GPA: 3.82 SAT (ERW): 570-660 SAT (M): 550-680 ACT (C): 25-30 ED: No	Admit Rate: 66% Undergrad Enrollment: 3,122 Total Enrollment: 4,353	BFA Fine Arts, emphases: Drawing, Painting	Portfolio req.
School of Visual Arts (SVA) 209 East 23rd Street, New York, NY 10010	GPA: 3.91 SAT (ERW): 545-650 SAT (M): 530-680 ACT (C): 23-27 ED: No	Overall College Admit Rate: 72% Undergrad Enrollment: 3,192 Total Enrollment: 3,692	BFA Fine Arts, concentrations: Drawing, Painting	Portfolio req.
SUNY Buffalo 285 Alumni Arena, North Campus, Buffalo, New York 14260	GPA: 3.7 SAT (ERW): 560-640 SAT (M): 580-670 ACT (C): 23-29 ED: No	Overall College Admit Rate: 37% Undergrad Enrollment: 22,306 Total Enrollment: 32,347	BFA Fine Arts, concentrations: General Studio, Painting	Portfolio req.

School	Avg. GPA, SAT Evidence-Based Reading Writing (ERW), SAT Math (M), and ACT Composite (C) Early Decision (ED): Yes/No	Admission Statistics	Program(s)	Portfolio Required (req.)
Syracuse University 401 University Place, Syracuse, NY 13244-2130	GPA: 3.67 SAT (ERW): N/A SAT (M): N/A ACT (C): N/A ED: Yes	Overall College Admit Rate: 69% Undergrad Enrollment: 14,479 Total Enrollment: 21,322	BFA Studio Arts, emphases: Drawing, Painting, Two Dimensional Studies	Portfolio req.
Arcadia University 450 S Easton Rd, Glenside, PA 19038	GPA: 3.7 SAT (ERW): 520-630 SAT (M): 510-600 ACT (C): 20-28 ED: No	Overall College Admit Rate: 74% Undergrad Enrollment: 2,014 Total Enrollment: 3,300	BFA Art, concentration: Painting	Portfolio req.
Pennsylvania Academy of Fine Arts (PAFA) 118-128 North Broad Street, Philadelphia, PA 19102	GPA: N/A SAT (ERW): N/A* SAT (M): N/A* ACT (C): N/A* *Test-optional ED: No	Overall College Admit Rate: 88% Undergrad Enrollment: 135 Total Enrollment: 188	BFA Drawing BFA Painting	Portfolio req.
Temple University 1801 N Broad St, Philadelphia, PA 19122	GPA: 3.48 SAT (ERW): N/A* SAT (M): N/A* ACT (C): N/A* *Test-optional ED: No	Overall College Admit Rate: 71% Undergrad Enrollment: 27,306 Total Enrollment: 37,236	BFA Painting	Portfolio req.

NORTHEAST

DRAWING & PAINTING PROGRAMS

School	Avg. GPA, SAT Evidence-Based Reading Writing (ERW), SAT Math (M), and ACT Composite (C) Early Decision (ED): Yes/No	Admission Statistics	Program(s)	Portfolio Required (req.)
Providence College 1 Cunningham Square, Providence, RI 02918	GPA: N/A SAT (ERW): 610-680 SAT (M): 600-680 ACT (C): 27-31 ED: Yes	Admit Rate: 54% Undergrad Enrollment: 4,298 Total Enrollment: 4,821	BA Studio Art, concentrations: Drawing, Painting	Portfolio optional
Rhode Island School of Design (RISD) 2 College St, Providence, RI 02903	GPA: N/A SAT (ERW): 610-700 SAT (M): 640-770 ACT (C): 27-32 ED: Yes	Admit Rate: 27% Undergrad Enrollment: 1,736 Total Enrollment: 2,227	BFA Painting, concentration: Drawing	Portfolio req.

YALE UNIVERSITY

Address: 220 York Street, Room 102, New Haven, CT 06511
Website: *https://www.art.yale.edu/about/study-areas/undergraduate-studies*
Contact: *https://www.yale.edu/contact-us*
Phone: (203) 432-4771
Email: student.questions@yale.edu

COST OF ATTENDANCE:

Tuition & Fees: $59,950 | **Additional Expenses:** $21,625
Total: $81,575

Financial Aid: https://www.yale.edu/admissions/financial-aid

ADDITIONAL INFORMATION:

Available Degree(s)

- BA Art, specialization: Painting/Printmaking

Portfolio Requirement

Portfolios are not required for incoming students. However, students must undergo the Sophomore Review as an undergraduate to continue on with the major. Applicants may submit an optional supplemental art portfolio.

Scholarships Offered

Yale scholarships are grants that are solely need-based. Merit-based scholarships are funded by external organizations or private companies. Yale does not require students, whose parents earn less than $65,000 annually, to contribute toward educational costs. Students whose families earn more than $150,000 may qualify for financial aid.

Special Opportunities

Art undergraduates at Yale are required to complete a senior project and participate in the Thesis Show, where they showcase their work. Art students are also in shared classrooms with Computing and the Arts majors. This major requires half of the coursework to be in computer science, and the other half in the arts.

Notable Alumni

Michele Abeles, Ann Agee, Kristin Baker, Gideon Bok, Chuck Close, Susanna Coffey, Njideka Akunyili Crosby, E.V. Day, Trisha Donnelly, Robert Engman, Tom Everhart, Walter S. Feldman, Mary Frey, Jan Gelb, Nancy Graves, Lily Harmon, Camille Hoff man, Tomashi Jackson, Joan Kahn, Lisa Kereszi, Austin Lee, Kate Levant, Tala Madani, Robert Mangold, Tameka Norris, Arthur Okamura, Jennifer Packer, Stephen Posen, Christina Quarles, Irwin Rubin, Matt Saunders, Hrvoje Slovenc, KaMan Tse, Jaret Vadera, Irene Weir, Garson Yu, and Jirayr Zorthian

CONNECTICUT

MAINE

MASSACHUSETTS

NEW HAMPSHIRE

NEW JERSEY

NEW YORK

PENNSYLVANIA

RHODE ISLAND

VERMONT

BOSTON UNIVERSITY

Address: 855 Commonwealth Avenue, Boston, MA 02215
Website: *https://www.bu.edu/cfa/undergraduate-painting/*
Contact: *https://www.bu.edu/about/contact-us/*
Phone: (617) 353-3350
Email: admissions@bu.edu

COST OF ATTENDANCE:

Tuition & Fees: $58,560 | **Additional Expenses:** $21,046
Total: $79,606

Financial Aid: http://www.bu.edu/finaid/

ADDITIONAL INFORMATION:

Available Degree(s)

- BFA Painting

Portfolio Requirement

Portfolios are required for incoming students. Submit 15-20 works via SlideRoom. At least three of the works must be created from observation.

Scholarships Offered

Boston University offers merit-based and need-based aid to all incoming students. Some of the merit scholarships for incoming students include the Trustee Scholarship (full tuition and fees), the Presidential Scholarship ($25,000 annually), the National Merit Scholarship (for National Merit finalists, valued at $25,000 per year), among many others. Need-based aid may come from the BU Grant, the BU Community Service Award, the Charles River Housing Grant, the Richard D. Cohen Scholarship (need and merit-based), or the Alumni Council Scholarship ($2,500).

Special Opportunities

Boston University's BFA in Painting emphasizes rigorous studio activity. Students explore approaches to painting to determine their personal styles. In their Junior year onwards, students are assigned private studios. Facilities are spacious and have views of the Charles River. Students also have access to the wood shop, spray room, black-and-white darkrooms, and equipment for ceramics, welding, and more. Students may also access BU's Printmaking facilities.

Notable Alumni

Mathew Cerletty, Joel Christian Gill, Brice Marden, Howardena Pindell, Christian Roman, and Pat Steir

CONNECTICUT

MAINE

MASSACHUSETTS

NEW HAMPSHIRE

NEW JERSEY

NEW YORK

PENNSYLVANIA

RHODE ISLAND

VERMONT

NORTHEAST

CONNECTICUT

MAINE

MASSACHUSETTS

NEW HAMPSHIRE

NEW JERSEY

NEW YORK

PENNSYLVANIA

RHODE ISLAND

VERMONT

MASSACHUSETTS COLLEGE OF ART & DESIGN (MASSART)

Address: 621 Huntington Ave, Boston, MA 02115
Website: *https://massart.edu/degree-programs/painting-bfa*
Contact: *https://massart.edu/contactus*
Phone: (617) 879-7000
Email: admissions@massart.edu

COST OF ATTENDANCE:

In-State Tuition & Fees: $14,200 | **Additional Expenses:** $19,200
Total: $33,400

New England Resident: $31,800 | **Additional Expenses:** $19,200
Total: $51,000

Out-of-State Tuition & Fees: $39,800 | **Additional Expenses:** $19,200
Total: $59,000

Financial Aid: https://massart.edu/financial-aid

ADDITIONAL INFORMATION:

Available Degree(s)

- BFA Painting

Portfolio Requirement
Portfolios are required for incoming students. Submit 15-20 examples of best and most recent work via the Common App. Applicants must not include artwork that copies another artist's work. Creative writing, screenplays, musical recordings, and theater performances are not allowed either.

Scholarships Offered
All eligible applicants are automatically considered for merit scholarships. To be considered, students need to demonstrate high academic achievement and showcase a strong portfolio. Out-of-state applicants may be eligible for the MassArt Merit Scholarship, the MassArt Transfer Merit Scholarship, or the Trustees Scholarship (covers all tuition and fees, renewable for four years). In-state applicants may be considered for the MassArt Merit Scholarship, the MassArt Transfer Merit Scholarship, and the Senator Paul E. Tsongas Scholarship (covers all tuition and fees for four years).

Special Opportunities
Drawing is a foundational part of the Painting curriculum. Coursework is crafted to specifically hone the link between drawing to form the basis of painting. Students learn basic and advanced techniques and learn how to develop their personal style via experimentation with form and content. Studio work is heavily emphasized, and students are expected to be dedicated to their studio work outside of class hours.

Notable Alumni
Henry Botkin, Robert Cumming, Americo DiFranza, Robert Ferrandini, Karen Frostig, Arne Glimcher, Paul Goodnight, William Gunn, Neil Jenney, John McNamara, Corrina Mensoff, Lewis Mutty, Richard Phillips, Sonya Rapoport, David Rose, Mimi Smith, May Stevens, Andrew Stevovich, William Wegman, Jackie Winsor, and Jean Zallinger

RUTGERS, THE STATE UNIVERSITY OF NEW JERSEY

Address: 2 Chapel Drive, New Brunswick, NJ 08901
Website: *https://www.masongross.rutgers.edu/degrees-programs/art-design/programs/bfa/#visual-arts*
Contact: *https://www.masongross.rutgers.edu/admissions/contact*
Phone: (848) 932-5241
Email: admissions@ugadm.rutgers.edu

COST OF ATTENDANCE:

In-State Tuition & Fees: $16,010 | **Additional Expenses:** $20,257
Total: $36,267

Out-of-State Tuition & Fees: $33,082 | **Additional Expenses:** $20,769
Total: $53,851

Financial Aid: https://financialaid.rutgers.edu/

ADDITIONAL INFORMATION:

Available Degree(s)

- BFA Visual Arts, concentrations: Drawing or Painting
- BA Art, concentration: Painting & Drawing

Portfolio Requirement

Portfolios are required for incoming students, for both degrees. Submit 15-20 works created within the past two years. Include at least one sketchbook page and a variety of media, such as observational drawings, paintings, print, or sculpture.

Scholarships Offered

Scholarships are awarded on a rolling basis, based on fund availability.

Special Opportunities

Students in the BFA Visual Arts program have six concentrations to choose from. They must complete three, year-long studio courses and complete seminars within their chosen area. Their concentration may be declared at their sophomore review. Students may do a double or hybrid concentration with faculty approval. The BA weaves in a liberal arts education with an interdisciplinary art approach.

Notable Alumni

Emma Amos, Allan Kaprow, Melissa Potter, George Segal, Joan Snyder, and Stephen Westfall

CONNECTICUT

MAINE

MASSACHUSETTS

NEW HAMPSHIRE

NEW JERSEY

NEW YORK

PENNSYLVANIA

RHODE ISLAND

VERMONT

NORTHEAST

CONNECTICUT

MAINE

MASSACHUSETTS

NEW HAMPSHIRE

NEW JERSEY

NEW YORK

PENNSYLVANIA

RHODE ISLAND

VERMONT

BARD COLLEGE

Address: 30 Campus Road, Annandale-on-Hudson, NY 12504
Website: *https://studioarts.bard.edu/*
Contact: *https://www.bard.edu/admission/contact/*
Phone: (845) 758-7472
Email: admissions@bard.edu

COST OF ATTENDANCE:

Tuition & Fees: $57,498 | **Additional Expenses:** $17,455
Total: $74,953

Financial Aid: https://www.bard.edu/financialaid/

ADDITIONAL INFORMATION:

Available Degree(s)

- BA Studio Arts

Portfolio Requirement

There is no portfolio requirement for incoming students. However, there is an optional supplemental submission.

Scholarships Offered

All scholarships at Bard are merit-based and need-based. Students are automatically considered for these rewards when they submit their university application. Scholarships include the Civic Engagement Scholarship, the President's Scholarship, the Bard Scholarship, and more.

Special Opportunities

At the end of the second year, students must present their work to a panel of faculty judges that will critique the student's body of work thus far. After passing the moderation process, students may take Level III coursework in advanced painting, drawing, sculpture, installation, and printmaking techniques. Seniors must complete a senior project and present their work at an open exhibition.

Notable Alumni

Robert C. Bassler, Sadie Benning, Cecilia Berkovic, Nayland Blake, Paul Chan, Ronald Chase, Frances Bean Cobain, Adriana Farmiga, Joanne Greenbaum, Daniel Gordon, David Horvitz, Jamie Livingston, Mary Lum, Malerie Marder, Lothar Osterburg, Serkan Ozkaya, R.H. Quaytman, Kristin Schattenfield-Rein, Carolee Schneeman, Amy Sillman Xaviera Simmons, Gordon Stevenson, and Rudi Stern

COLUMBIA UNIVERSITY

Address: 1130 Amsterdam Avenue, New York, NY 10027
Website: *https://arts.columbia.edu/undergraduate-visual-arts-program*
Contact: *https://undergrad.admissions.columbia.edu/contact*
Phone: (212) 854-2522
Email: ugrad-ask@columbia.edu

COST OF ATTENDANCE:

Tuition & Fees: $63,530 | **Additional Expenses:** $19,054
Total: $82,584

Financial Aid: https://www.sfs.columbia.edu/fin-aid

ADDITIONAL INFORMATION:

Available Degree(s)

- BA Visual Arts, concentrations: Drawing or Painting

Portfolio Requirement

Portfolios are not required for incoming students. However, Columbia accepts optional creative supplements.

Scholarships Offered

Columbia University offers need-based aid. They also offer fellowships to students from specific backgrounds.

Special Opportunities

The Visual Arts program at Columbia is interdisciplinary. Students explore various forms of visual expression. They also learn techniques while enhancing their analytical voice. Undergraduates in this program may choose a concentration in Drawing, Painting, Sculpture, Photography, Printmaking, or Video. They may combine any of these disciplines as well.

Notable Alumni

Charles Alston, Irene Aronson, Caitlin Cherry, Ismail Gulgee, James Hewlett, Rockwell Kent, Edward Koren, Agnes Martin, Georgia O'Keeffe, Ad Reinhardt, Dana Schutz, Burton Silverman, and James Perry Wilson

CONNECTICUT

MAINE

MASSACHUSETTS

NEW HAMPSHIRE

NEW JERSEY

NEW YORK

PENNSYLVANIA

RHODE ISLAND

VERMONT

NORTHEAST

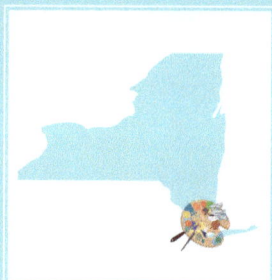

THE COOPER UNION

Address: 30 Cooper Sq, New York, NY 10003
Website: *https://cooper.edu/art/curriculum*
Contact: *https://cooper.edu/admissions/contact*
Phone: (212) 353-4120
Email: admissions@cooper.edu

COST OF ATTENDANCE:

Tuition & Fees: $46,820 | **Additional Expenses:** $22,302
Total: $69,122

Financial Aid: https://cooper.edu/admissions/financial-aid

ADDITIONAL INFORMATION:

Available Degree(s)

- BFA Art

Portfolio Requirement

Portfolios are required for incoming students. Applicants must submit a supplemental Hometest. Instructions appear in the applicant portal after submission of the application. A portfolio and sketchbook must also be submitted with the Hometest.

Scholarships Offered

Cooper Union offers various fellowships and funds for students from specific educational, disciplinary, geographical, or ethnic backgrounds. Awards vary in amount.

Special Opportunities

Students in the BFA Art program start by completing the Foundation Program in their first year. The foundational program focuses on exploring 2D, 3D, and 4D projects, concepts and principles of art, and various techniques. Students become critical thinkers through theory and history of art courses as well. In the second year, students may choose courses within a discipline of focus, whether that be drawing, painting, printmaking, sculpture, graphic design, photography, or audiovisual art. Students gain increasing freedom and flexibility in their third year. By the last year, seniors showcase their work at the Senior Presentation.

Notable Alumni

Donald Baechler, Renata Bernal, Anna Conway, Will Cotton, Eric Drooker, Robert Feintuch, Irving Fierstein, Minetta Good, William Harnett, R.B. Kitaj, Lee Krasner, Kathleen Kucka, Charles E. Pont, Arnold Alfred Schmidt, George Segal, Emily McGary Selinger, Philip Taaffe, Jovan Karlo Villalba, Tom Wesselmann, Pennerton West, Jack Whitten, Jerome Witkin, Dan Witz, and Sarah A. Worden

CONNECTICUT

MAINE

MASSACHUSETTS

NEW HAMPSHIRE

NEW JERSEY

NEW YORK

PENNSYLVANIA

RHODE ISLAND

VERMONT

CUNY HUNTER COLLEGE

Address: 695 Park Ave, New York, NY 10065
Website: *https://huntercollegeart.org/bfa-program/*
Contact: *http://www.hunter.cuny.edu/admissions/*
undergraduateadmissions/contactus
Phone: (212) 772-4490
Email: admissions@hunter.cuny.edu

COST OF ATTENDANCE:

In-State Tuition & Fees: $6,930 | **Additional Expenses:** $20,478
Total: $27,408

Out-of-State Tuition & Fees: $18,600 | **Additional Expenses:** $20,478
Total: $39,078

Financial Aid: https://hunter.cuny.edu/students/financial-aid/

ADDITIONAL INFORMATION:

Available Degree(s)

- BFA Studio Art, concentrations: Drawing or Painting

Portfolio Requirement

Portfolios are not required for incoming students. However they
may be at some point along the BFA program.

Scholarships Offered

CUNY Hunter College offers the Guttman Transfer Scholarships and
the William E. Macaulay Honors Program. Students must complete
the FAFSA to be considered for these scholarships. Hunter College
students may also apply for applications such as the Freshman
Honors Scholar Program, International Student Scholarships, and
more. A FAFSA is required each year.

Special Opportunities

The CUNY Hunter BFA program is a fifth-year program, meaning that
it takes, on average, five years to complete. The extra year is meant
to serve as an opportunity for an in-depth focus into studio practice,
contemporary art, and theoretical issues. The program culminates
in a BFA Degree Show. Students learn about all phases of creating
an exhibition, and are involved in tasks such as lighting, labeling,
designing, installation, planning, and scheduling the event.

Notable Alumni

Echo Eggebrecht, Denise Green, Kathleen Kucka, and Dan Walsh

CONNECTICUT

MAINE

MASSACHUSETTS

NEW HAMPSHIRE

NEW JERSEY

NEW YORK

PENNSYLVANIA

RHODE ISLAND

VERMONT

NORTHEAST

CONNECTICUT

MAINE

MASSACHUSETTS

NEW HAMPSHIRE

NEW JERSEY

NEW YORK

PENNSYLVANIA

RHODE ISLAND

VERMONT

PARSONS - THE NEW SCHOOL

Address: 66 Fifth Avenue, New York, NY 10011
Website: *https://www.newschool.edu/parsons/bfa-fine-arts/*
Contact: *https://www.newschool.edu/parsons/contact/*
Phone: (212) 229-8900
Email: thinkparsons@newschool.edu

COST OF ATTENDANCE:

Tuition & Fees: $51,722 | **Additional Expenses:** N/A
Total: $51,722

Financial Aid: https://www.newschool.edu/financial-aid/

ADDITIONAL INFORMATION:

Available Degree(s)

- BFA Fine Arts

Portfolio Requirement

Portfolios are required for incoming students. Applicants must complete the Parsons Challenge, a new visual work inspired by a theme set by the university. Applicants must also submit 8-12 works. Submit via SlideRoom.

Scholarships Offered

The New School offers merit-based and need-based aid to students. Students are automatically considered for merit-based scholarships. These are based on the strength of the application and portfolio. Need-based aid is available to students who are eligible and submit the FAFSA.

Special Opportunities

BFA Fine Arts students at Parsons study painting, drawing, sculpture, and 4D media. They also have access and proximity to museums, art galleries, internships, and other opportunities to engage with artists and network. Students are encouraged to study abroad to gain new perspectives. Study abroad opportunities are in Paris, London, Florence, and more.

Notable Alumni

Kevin Appel, Louisa Bertman, Ilse Bischoff, Rosemary Cove, Peter DeSeve, Leo and Diane Dillon, Jane Frank, Adolph Gottlieb, Julia Gran, Bessie Pease Gutmann, Julie Harvey, Hidekaz Himaruya, Edward Hopper, Steffani Jemison, Jasper Johns, Shirley Kaneda, Sol Kjok, Dimitar Lukanov, Rob Pruitt, Bob Rafei, Joel Resnicoff, Andrew Cornell Robinson, Norman Rockwell, Anrika Rupp, Gavin Spielman, Emily Sundblad, Rodel Tapaya, Julie Umerle, Ai Weiwei, Nick van Woert, Betsy Wolfston, Brian Wood, Dan Yaccarino, and Janise Yntema

PRATT INSTITUTE

Address: 200 Willoughby Avenue, Brooklyn, NY 11205
Website: *https://www.pratt.edu/academics/school-of-art/undergraduate-school-of-art/undergraduate-fine-arts/*
Contact: *https://www.pratt.edu/academics/school-of-design/undergraduate-school-of-design/fashion/fashion-department-contact/*
Phone: (718) 636-3600
Email: admissions@pratt.edu

COST OF ATTENDANCE:

Tuition & Fees: $53,566 | **Additional Expenses:** $19,824
Total: $73,390

Financial Aid: https://www.pratt.edu/admissions/financing-your-education/financing-undergraduate/

ADDITIONAL INFORMATION:

Available Degree(s)

- BFA Fine Arts, emphases: Drawing or Painting

Portfolio Requirement

Portfolios are required for incoming students. Submit 12-20 drawings of your most recent work. Students must include 3-5 drawings from observation. Submit via SlideRoom.

Scholarships Offered

Pratt offers merit-based and endowed scholarships in addition to need-based grants. Furthermore, there are merit-based scholarships available to international students as well. The Presidential Merit-Based Scholarships are available to all Pratt students in varied award amounts.

Special Opportunities

In the first year, Fine Arts students take foundational studio coursework and liberal arts classes. In the second year, students continue with liberal arts coursework and start taking courses more focused in their areas of emphasis. Electives are taken in the third and fourth years. Examples of available electives include charcoal drawing, bronze casting, etching and ceramics, new media, and more. The program culminates in a thesis and an exhibition of their work on campus.

Notable Alumni

Imna Arroyo, Leigh Behnke, Trudy Benson, Willard Bond, Kenneth Browne, Louis Delsarte, Félix González-Torres, Eva Hesse, Jim Hodges, Ellsworth Kelly, Jacob Lawrence, Robert Mapplethorpe, Roxy Paine, Dennis Peterson, David Ratcliff, Nicholas Reale, Edna Reindel, Willy Bo Richardson, Mario Robinson, Stefan Sagmeister, Jenny Scobel, Joan Semmel, Susan Louise Shatter, Salman Toor, Max Weber, Kent Williams, William T. Williams, Terry Winters, and Robert Yasuda

CONNECTICUT

MAINE

MASSACHUSETTS

NEW HAMPSHIRE

NEW JERSEY

NEW YORK

PENNSYLVANIA

RHODE ISLAND

VERMONT

NORTHEAST

CONNECTICUT

MAINE

MASSACHUSETTS

NEW HAMPSHIRE

NEW JERSEY

NEW YORK

PENNSYLVANIA

RHODE ISLAND

VERMONT

SCHOOL OF VISUAL ARTS (SVA)

Address: 209 East 23rd Street, New York, NY 10010
Website: *https://sva.edu/academics/undergraduate/bfa-fine-arts*
Contact: *https://sva.edu/contact-and-map*
Phone: (212) 592- 2100
Email: admissions@sva.edu

COST OF ATTENDANCE:

Tuition & Fees: $49,750 | **Additional Expenses:** N/A
Total: $49,750

Financial Aid: https://sva.edu/admissions/financial-resources/financial-aid

ADDITIONAL INFORMATION:

Available Degree(s)

- BFA Fine Arts, concentrations: Drawing or Painting

Portfolio Requirement

Portfolios are required for incoming students. Submit 15-20 works via SlideRoom.

Scholarships Offered

The Silad H. Rhodes Scholarship is available to students of all majors with an unlisted award amount. Students with a GPA of 3.0+ are eligible. First-time freshmen applicants must submit all application materials by February to be considered. There is no separate application.

Special Opportunities

SVA is located within walking distance of many world-famous museums and galleries. Facilities include wood and metal shops, ceramics, the Fine Arts Bio Art Lab, a printmaking lab, as well as sound and fibers studios. Seniors showcase their artwork at Open Studios, which dealers and curators attend. It is an opportunity for students to network with professionals in the field. Off-site workshops are also held in metal casting, neon, glass-making, and large-scale ceramics.

Notable Alumni

Kesewa Aboah, Esao Andrews, Ali Banisadr, Samuel Bayer, Robert Beauchamp, Tom Burr, Robin Byrd, Rosson Crow, Inka Essenhigh, Neck Face, Charles Fazzino, Andrea Fraser, Pamela Fraser, Barnaby Furnas, Jedd Garet, Rita Genet, Kate Gilmore, Keith Haring, Jane hart, gus Heinze, Reverend Jen, Vashtie Kola, Joseph Kosuth, Tina La Porta, Robert Lazzarini, Dinh Q. Lê, Sol LeWitt, Jennifer Macdonald, Donald Martiny, Mark McCoy, Aleksandra Mir, Steve Mumford, Paul A. Paddock, Elizabeth Peyton, Andrew Cornell Robinson, Jorge Luis Rodriguez, Brian Rutenberg, Kenny Scharf, Jeff Sonhouse, Sarah Sze, John von Bergen, and Charlie White

SUNY BUFFALO

Address: 285 Alumni Arena, North Campus, Buffalo, New York 14260
Website: *https://arts-sciences.buffalo.edu/art/undergraduate/bfa.html*
Contact: *https://admissions.buffalo.edu/contact/*
Phone: (716) 645-6900
Email: ub-admissions@buffalo.edu

COST OF ATTENDANCE

In-State Tuition & Fees: $7,270 | **Additional Expenses:** $39,066
Total: $46,336

Out-of-State Tuition & Fees: $24,740.00 | **Additional Expenses:** $4126
Total: $28,866

Financial Aid: https://financialaid.buffalo.edu/

ADDITIONAL INFORMATION:

Available Degree(s)

- BFA Fine Arts, concentrations: General Studio or Painting

Portfolio Requirement

Portfolios are not required for incoming students. However, there may be a portfolio review at some point during the undergraduate studies.

Scholarships Offered

University at Buffalo offers various merit-based and need-based scholarships and grants including the Presidential Scholarship and the Provost Scholarship.

Special Opportunities

The studio art labs at SUNY Buffalo are spacious and support digital and experimental techniques. The campus houses a biological arts laboratory, an electronics art lab, galleries, digital and multimedia labs, analog photography labs, printmaking labs, an audio lab, and a sculpture facility. They also house technology such as laser cutters, CNC routers, and one of the largest university foundries in the East Coast.

Notable Alumni

Allan D'Arcangelo, Sylvia Lark, and Alberto Rey

CONNECTICUT

MAINE

MASSACHUSETTS

NEW HAMPSHIRE

NEW JERSEY

NEW YORK

PENNSYLVANIA

RHODE ISLAND

VERMONT

NORTHEAST

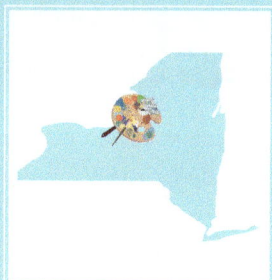

CONNECTICUT

MAINE

MASSACHUSETTS

NEW HAMPSHIRE

NEW JERSEY

NEW YORK

PENNSYLVANIA

RHODE ISLAND

VERMONT

SYRACUSE UNIVERSITY

Address: 202 Crouse College, Syracuse, NY 13244
Website: *https://vpa.syr.edu/academics/art/programs/studio-arts-bfa/*
Contact: *https://www.syracuse.edu/admissions/undergraduate/contact/*
Phone: (315) 443-2769
Email: admissu@syr.edu

COST OF ATTENDANCE:

Tuition & Fees: $57,591 | **Additional Expenses:** $44,448.8
Total: $80,039.80

Financial Aid: https://www.syracuse.edu/admissions/cost-and-aid/

ADDITIONAL INFORMATION:

Available Degree(s)

- BFA Studio Arts, emphases: Drawing, Painting, or Two Dimensional Studies

Portfolio Requirement

Portfolios are required for incoming students. Submit 12-20 recent works. Syracuse University strongly suggests that at least six drawings are from observation.

Scholarships Offered

Syracuse University offers various merit-based and need-based scholarships and grants. The 1870 Scholarship covers full tuition for the full length of the undergraduate program. Artistic Scholarships are awarded to students based on talent and a maintained cumulative GPA of 2.75+.

Special Opportunities

Syracuse University offers the VPA Study Abroad experience for art majors. Studio Art majors frequently go to Florence, Italy for their study abroad experience.

Notable Alumni

James Bishop, Birgitta Moran Farmer, Frances Farrand Dodge, Joseph S. Kozlowski, Mark Lombardi, Jim Ridlon, and Kate Vrijmoet

ARCADIA UNIVERSITY

Address: 450 S Easton Rd, Glenside, PA 19038
Website: *https://www.arcadia.edu/academics/programs/art-bfa*
Contact: *https://www.arcadia.edu/admissions*
Phone: (877) 272-2342
Email: https://www.arcadia.edu/admissions

COST OF ATTENDANCE:

Tuition & Fees: $46,430 | **Additional Expenses:** $16,030
Total: $62,460

Financial Aid: https://www.arcadia.edu/admissions/financial-aid-scholarships

ADDITIONAL INFORMATION:

Available Degree(s)

- BFA Art, concentration: Painting

Portfolio Requirement

Portfolios are required for incoming students. Submit 10-20 works via SlideRoom along with a 250-500-word statement. Drawings from observation are strongly encouraged.

Scholarships Offered

Arcadia University offers merit and need-based scholarships. All of their merit scholarships are automatically renewable year to year as long as the student remains in good academic standing. Scholarships include the Arcadia University Distinguished Scholarship, the Achievement Award, the Portfolio Review Award, and more. Awards range from $1,000 to $28,000 per year.

Special Opportunities

Arcadia University holds small, interactive art classes. Students participate in hands-on apprenticeships and have the opportunity to study abroad. Students are prepared for graduate study in studio art, as exhibiting artists, or for entry-level positions within the art industry. Some concentrations require an internship or apprenticeship.

Notable Alumni

Abbey Ryan

CONNECTICUT

MAINE

MASSACHUSETTS

NEW HAMPSHIRE

NEW JERSEY

NEW YORK

PENNSYLVANIA

RHODE ISLAND

VERMONT

NORTHEAST

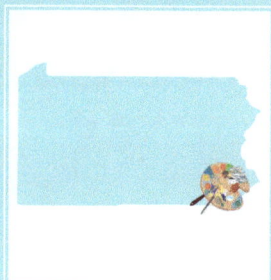

CONNECTICUT

MAINE

MASSACHUSETTS

NEW HAMPSHIRE

NEW JERSEY

NEW YORK

PENNSYLVANIA

RHODE ISLAND

VERMONT

PENNSYLVANIA ACADEMY OF FINE ARTS (PAFA)

Address: 118-128 North Broad Street, Philadelphia, PA 19102
Website: *https://www.pafa.org/school/academics/areas-study-departments/drawing*
Contact: *https://www.pafa.org/about*
Phone: (215) 972-7600
Email: info@pafa.org

COST OF ATTENDANCE:

Tuition & Fees: $36,058 | **Additional Expenses:** $23,204
Total: $59,262

Financial Aid: https://www.pafa.org/school/admissions/financing-your-education/types-financial-aid

ADDITIONAL INFORMATION:

Available Degree(s)

- BFA Drawing
- BFA Painting

Portfolio Requirement

Portfolios are required for incoming students. Submit 12-15 images via Slideroom.

Scholarships Offered

According to PAFA, 100% of their students receive merit scholarships. The average award is $19,722. Merit-based and need-based aid is available to all students.

Special Opportunities

Drawing students build strong technical skills at PAFA. Students are encouraged to build their personal style and ideas. They learn cast drawing, figure drawing, still life, basic and advanced rendering skills, and media such as pencil, charcoal, and mixed-media approaches.

In the painting program, students explore classical representation, abstraction, and observational painting. All students receive a private studio and workspace.

Notable Alumni

Robert Beck, Sarah Blakeslee, Thomas Hill, Marie Hull, Elsa Jemne, Grace Spaulding John, and Alice Kindler

TEMPLE UNIVERSITY

Address: 1801 N Broad St, Philadelphia, PA 19122
Website: *https://tyler.temple.edu/programs/painting*
Contact: *https://www.temple.edu/contact/*
Phone: (215) 204-7000
Email: askanowl@temple.edu

COST OF ATTENDANCE:

In-State Tuition & Fees: $18,168 | **Additional Expenses:** $17,880
Total: $36,048

Out-of-State Tuition & Fees: $31,440 | **Additional Expenses:** $19,944
Total: $51,384

Financial Aid: https://admissions.temple.edu/costs-aid-scholarships/financial-aid-scholarships

ADDITIONAL INFORMATION:

Available Degree(s)

- BFA Painting

Portfolio Requirement

Portfolios are required for incoming students. Submit via SlideRoom.

Scholarships Offered

All students who submit their application by February 1 are automatically considered for merit scholarships. Award amounts range from $1,000 to full tuition.

Special Opportunities

At Temple University's Tyler School of Art and Architecture, painting students have access to more than 18,000 square feet of studio space specifically designed for painting and drawing. The campus houses six top-floor studio rooms with floor-to-ceiling windows and ample light. Students frequently study abroad at Temple Rome or in Venice to learn about the cultural, historical, and global contexts of art.

Notable Alumni

Laura Marie Greenwood, Trenton Doyle Hancock, Andrew Hussie, Simmie Knox, Nicholas Muellner, Ralph Rucci, Paula Scher, Sarai Sherman, Aaron Shikler, and Jen Simmons

CONNECTICUT

MAINE

MASSACHUSETTS

NEW HAMPSHIRE

NEW JERSEY

NEW YORK

PENNSYLVANIA

RHODE ISLAND

VERMONT

NORTHEAST

CONNECTICUT

MAINE

MASSACHUSETTS

NEW HAMPSHIRE

NEW JERSEY

NEW YORK

PENNSYLVANIA

RHODE ISLAND

VERMONT

PROVIDENCE COLLEGE

Address: 1 Cunningham Square, Providence, RI 02918
Website: *https://art.providence.edu/studio-art/drawing/*
Contact: *https://admission.providence.edu/contact/*
Phone: (401) 865-1000
Email: pcadmiss@providence.edu

COST OF ATTENDANCE:

Tuition & Fees: $55,850 | **Additional Expenses:** $18,522
Total: $74,372

Financial Aid: https://financial-aid.providence.edu/

ADDITIONAL INFORMATION:

Available Degree(s)

- BA Studio Art, concentrations: Drawing or Painting

Portfolio Requirement

Portfolios are not required for incoming students. However, they are optional.

Scholarships Offered

Providence College offers merit-based tuition scholarships ranging from $20,000 to $35,000 per year. No separate application is required. Students are evaluated based on their application. Furthermore, Providence College offers the Fine Arts Tuition Scholarship, which judges students based on their portfolio work.

Special Opportunities

Students in the studio art program build upon a foundation of the fundamentals of visual art. They are taught 2D and 3D design and drawing. Concentrations include ceramics, digital imaging, drawing, painting, photography, printmaking, and sculpture. Art history is also required. In their senior year, students present a thesis exhibition and publish their work in the department's annual publication. Providence College offers a Business and Innovation Minor, which is popular among art students.

Notable Alumni

Stephan Brigidi, Samantha Cataldo, Stephen Forneris, Helena Gomez, Will Hutnick, Hannah Johnson, Mark Mazzenga, Molly O'Brien, Hendrick Paul, Mary Pelletier, Maura Reilly, Michael Rose, William Ruggiero, Althea Ruoppo, Eric Schofield, and Mary Tinti

RHODE ISLAND SCHOOL OF DESIGN (RISD)

Address: 2 College St, Providence, RI 02903
Website: *https://www.risd.edu/academics/painting/bachelors-program*
Contact: *https://www.risd.edu/academics/apparel-design/contact/*
Phone: (401) 454-6300
Email: admissions@risd.edu

COST OF ATTENDANCE:

Tuition & Fees: $55,220 | **Additional Expenses:** $22,060
Total: $77,280

Financial Aid: https://www.risd.edu/student-financial-services/undergraduate-aid/

ADDITIONAL INFORMATION:

Available Degree(s)

- BFA Painting, concentration: Drawing

Portfolio Requirement

Portfolios are required for incoming students. Submit 12-20 recent works via SlideRoom. Applicants are strongly encouraged to submit drawings from observation. Applicants must also complete The Assignment - a two-part portfolio requirement that involves a visual study based on a prompt.

Scholarships Offered

RISD scholarships are need-based. Students must submit a FAFSA application each year to be considered. RISD is also partnered with Scholarship Universe, a website that matches students with outside scholarships and keeps students on track with deadlines.

Special Opportunities

The Painting department is headquartered in a former 19th-century church designed by architect, Thomas Teft. Students get to experience this building along with a dedicated gallery for student work and well-lit, spacious studios. The RISD Museum is located next door for easy access to a collection of painting and sculpture from almost every period and global works. Students also have access to specimens in the Nature Lab.

Notable Alumni

Daniel Arango, David Bowes, Joe Bradley, Val Britton, Erin Castellan, Roz Chast, Emiko Davies, Christopher Denise, Liz Deschenes, Arthur Deshaies, John Dilg, Alex Dodge, Arthur Douglas, Nicole Eisenman, Shepard Fairey, Herbert Farnum, Jon Foster, Aaron Gilbert, Suzy González, Bruce Helander, Adam Helms, Jessica Hess, Håvard Homstvedt, Shara Hughes, Yvonne Jacquette, Jane Kim, Cynthia Lahti, Sonny Liew, Grace Lin, Jason Lutes, Fred Lynch, Julie Mehretu, Richard Merkin, Matt Mignanelli, D. Jeffrey Mims, Laura Owns, Sam Posey, Deborah Poynton, Francis Quirk, Anton Refregier, Antoine Revoy, Paolo Rivera, Clare Rojas, Schandra Singh, Sonya Sklaroff , Anne Spalter, Andrew Stevovich, Kurt Wenner, Mabel Woodward, William Woodward, Zio Zegler, and Pippi Zomoza

CONNECTICUT

MAINE

MASSACHUSETTS

NEW HAMPSHIRE

NEW JERSEY

NEW YORK

PENNSYLVANIA

RHODE ISLAND

VERMONT

NORTHEAST

ILLINOIS

INDIANA

IOWA

KANSAS

MICHIGAN

MINNESOTA

MISSOURI

NEBRASKA

NORTH DAKOTA

OHIO

SOUTH DAKOTA

WISCONSIN

CHAPTER 12

REGION TWO

MIDWEST

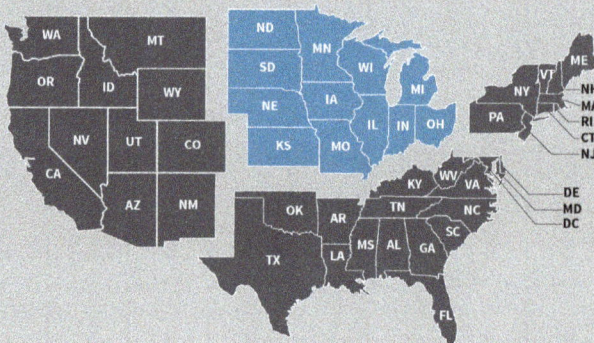

13 *Programs* | 12 *States*

1. *IL – American Academy of Art College*
2. *IL - Bradley University*
3. *IL - School of the Art Institute Chicago*
4. *IL - University of Illinois, Chicago*
5. *IL - University of Illinois Urbana-Champaign (UIUC)*
6. *IA - Drake University*
7. *MN - Minneapolis College of Art & Design*
8. *MN - University of Minnesota, Twin Cities*
9. *MO - College of the Ozarks*
10. *MO - Kansas City Art Institute*
11. *MO - Washington University, St. Louis*
12. *OH - Cleveland Institute of Art*
13. *OH - Ohio University*

DRAWING & PAINTING PROGRAMS

School	Avg. GPA, SAT Evidence-Based Reading Writing (ERW), SAT Math (M), and ACT Composite (C) Early Decision (ED): Yes/No	Admission Statistics	Program(s)	Portfolio Required (req.)
American Academy of Art College 332 Michigan Ave, Chicago, IL 60604	GPA: N/A SAT (ERW): N/A SAT (M): N/A ACT (C): N/A ED: No	Overall College Admit Rate: N/A Undergrad Enrollment: 169 Total Enrollment: 169	BFA Oil Painting BFA Watercolor Painting	Portfolio not req.
Bradley University 1501 W. Bradley Ave., Peoria, IL, 61625	GPA: 3.83 SAT (ERW): 540-630 SAT (M): 540-650 ACT (C): 22-28 ED: No	Overall College Admit Rate: 73% Undergrad Enrollment: 4,574 Total Enrollment: 5,855	BFA Studio Art, concentrations: Drawing or Painting	Portfolio not req.
School of the Art Institute of Chicago (SAIC) 36 S. Wabash Ave., Chicago, IL 60603	GPA: N/A SAT (ERW): 560-660 SAT (M): 480-600 ACT (C): 22-25 ED: No	Admit Rate: 78% Undergrad Enrollment: 2,487 Total Enrollment: 3,132	BFA Studio, area: Painting and Drawing	Portfolio req.
University of Illinois, Chicago 1200 W Harrison St, Chicago, IL 60607	GPA: N/A SAT (ERW): 510-610 SAT (M): 520-640 ACT (C): 21-29 ED: No	Overall College Admit Rate: 73% Undergrad Enrollment: 21,921 Total Enrollment: 33,518	BFA Art, concentration: Studio Arts	Portfolio req.

School	Avg. GPA, SAT Evidence-Based Reading Writing (ERW), SAT Math (M), and ACT Composite (C) Early Decision (ED): Yes/No	Admission Statistics	Program(s)	Portfolio Required (req.)
University of Illinois Urbana-Champaign (UIUC) 901 West Illinois Street, Urbana, IL 61801	GPA: N/A SAT (ERW): 590-700 SAT (M): 620-770 ACT (C): 27-33 ED: Yes	Overall College Admit Rate: 50% Undergrad Enrollment: 34,559 Total Enrollment: 56,257	BFA Studio Art, concentration: Painting BA Studio Art, concentration: Painting	Portfolio not req.
Drake University 2507 University Avenue, Des Moines, IA 50311	GPA: 3.7 SAT (ERW): 560-660 SAT (M): 550-680 ACT (C): 23-30 ED: No	Overall College Admit Rate: 68% Undergrad Enrollment: 2,848 Total Enrollment: 4,774	BFA Studio Art, concentrations: Drawing or Painting	Portfolio not req.
Minneapolis College of Art & Design 2501 Stevens Avenue, Minneapolis, MN 55404	GPA: N/A SAT (ERW): N/A* SAT (M): N/A* ACT (C): N/A* *Test-optional ED: No	Overall College Admit Rate: 55% Undergrad Enrollment: 670 Total Enrollment: 760	BFA Painting and Drawing BFA Fine Arts Studio	Portfolio req.
University of Minnesota, Twin Cities 330 21st Ave S., Minneapolis, MN 55455	GPA: N/A SAT (ERW): 600-700 SAT (M): 640-760 ACT (C): 25-31 ED: No	Overall College Admit Rate: 70% Undergrad Enrollment: 36,061 Total Enrollment: 52,017	BFA Art, concentration: Drawing, Painting, and Printmaking	Portfolio not req.

MIDWEST

DRAWING & PAINTING PROGRAMS

School	Avg. GPA, SAT Evidence-Based Reading Writing (ERW), SAT Math (M), and ACT Composite (C) Early Decision (ED): Yes/No	Admission Statistics	Program(s)	Portfolio Required (req.)
College of the Ozarks 100 Opportunity Ave, Point Lookout, MO 65726	GPA: 3.37 SAT (ERW): 470-540 SAT (M): 480-560 ACT (C): 18-23 ED: No	Overall College Admit Rate: 56% Undergrad Enrollment: 836 Total Enrollment: 836	BA Art, emphasis: Studio Art	Portfolio not req.
Kansas City Art Institute 4415 Warwick Blvd., Kansas City, MO 64111	GPA: N/A SAT (ERW): N/A* SAT (M): N/A* ACT (C): N/A* *Test-optional ED: No	Overall College Admit Rate: 59% Undergrad Enrollment: 698 Total Enrollment: 698	BFA Painting	Portfolio req.
Washington University in St. Louis 1 Brookings Dr, St. Louis, MO 63130	GPA: 4.21 SAT (ERW): 720-760 SAT (M): 760-800 ACT (C): 33-35 ED: Yes	Overall College Admit Rate: 16% Undergrad Enrollment: 7,653 Total Enrollment: 15,449	BFA Studio Art, area: Painting	Portfolio req.
Cleveland Institute of Art 11610 Euclid Avenue, Cleveland, OH 44106	GPA: N/A SAT (ERW): 560-680 SAT (M): 510-620 ACT (C): 19-27 ED: No	Overall College Admit Rate: 67% Undergrad Enrollment: 599 Total Enrollment: 599	BFA Drawing BFA Painting	Portfolio req.

School	Avg. GPA, SAT Evidence-Based Reading Writing (ERW), SAT Math (M), and ACT Composite (C) Early Decision (ED): Yes/No	Admission Statistics	Program(s)	Portfolio Required (req.)
Ohio University Ohio University, Athens, OH 45701	GPA: 3.55 SAT (ERW): 530-630 SAT (M): 520-620 ACT (C): 21-26 ED: No	Overall College Admit Rate: 87% Undergrad Enrollment: 19,284 Total Enrollment: 25,714	BFA Studio Art, concentration: Painting + Drawing	Portfolio req.

MIDWEST

ILLINOIS

INDIANA

IOWA

KANSAS

MICHIGAN

MINNESOTA

MISSOURI

NEBRASKA

NORTH DAKOTA

OHIO

SOUTH DAKOTA

WISCONSIN

AMERICAN ACADEMY OF ART COLLEGE

Address: 332 Michigan Ave, Chicago, IL 60604
Website: *https://www.aaart.edu/academics/oil-painting/*
Contact: *https://www.aaart.edu/*
Phone: (312) 461-0600
Email: info@aaart.edu

COST OF ATTENDANCE:

Tuition & Fees: $36,670 | **Additional Expenses:** $8,468
Total: $45,138

Financial Aid: https://www.aaart.edu/admissions/financial-aid/

ADDITIONAL INFORMATION:

Available Degree(s)

- BFA Oil Painting
- BFA Watercolor Painting

Portfolio Requirement

There is no portfolio requirement for incoming first-year students.

Scholarships Offered

American Academy of Art College highly encourages students to submit a FAFSA in order to receive federally-funded need-based aid. Students are also welcome to apply to external scholarships.

Special Opportunities

Students in both Oil Painting and Watercolor Painting take intensive studio coursework to learn the technical aspects of the medium. Class assignments serve to build the professional portfolio. Students apply critical, historical, and theoretical principles to their body of work.

Notable Alumni

Joyce Ballantyne, Thomas Blackshear, Sandy Dvore, Gil Elvgren, Rupert Kinnard, Richard Schmid, Richard Sloan, Haddon Sundblom, and Kanye West

BRADLEY UNIVERSITY

Address: 1501 W. Bradley Ave., Peoria, IL, 61625
Website: *https://www.bradley.edu/academic/departments/art/major/drawing/*
Contact: *https://www.bradley.edu/admissions/*
Phone: (309) 676-7611
Email: webmaster@bradley.edu

COST OF ATTENDANCE:

Tuition & Fees: $35,940 | **Additional Expenses:** $12,048
Total: $47,988

Financial Aid: https://www.bradley.edu/offices/student/sfs/financial-assistance/assistance/

ADDITIONAL INFORMATION:

Available Degree(s)

- BFA Studio Art, concentrations: Drawing or Painting

Portfolio Requirement

Portfolios are not required for incoming students. However, a portfolio review is mandatory after the first year for continuation with the BFA degree.

Scholarships Offered

Bradley University offers various need-based and merit-based scholarships. There are the Academic Scholarships, Legacy and Sibling Scholarships, Fine and Performing Arts Scholarships, the Civil Engineering and Construction Leadership Excellence Scholarship and more. The Academic Scholarships are the most common and range from $56,000-$96,000 over four years.

Special Opportunities

Students in the BFA program undergo intensive studio coursework to build upon their technical skills within their concentration, whether that be drawing or painting. Bradley University also offers a B.S. or a B.A. degree for students interested in learning art but having a more emphasized liberal arts background. Students frequently study abroad in London or Rome.

Notable Alumni

Bonny Pierce Lhotka

ILLINOIS

INDIANA

IOWA

KANSAS

MICHIGAN

MINNESOTA

MISSOURI

NEBRASKA

NORTH DAKOTA

OHIO

SOUTH DAKOTA

WISCONSIN

MIDWEST

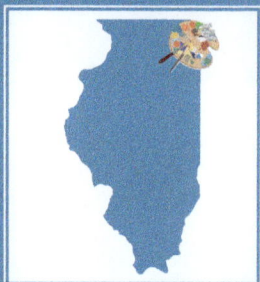

ILLINOIS

INDIANA

IOWA

KANSAS

MICHIGAN

MINNESOTA

MISSOURI

NEBRASKA

NORTH DAKOTA

OHIO

SOUTH DAKOTA

WISCONSIN

SCHOOL OF THE ART INSTITUTE OF CHICAGO (SAIC)

Address: 36 S. Wabash Ave., Chicago, IL 60603
Website: *https://www.saic.edu/academics/departments/painting-and-drawing*
Contact: *https://www.saic.edu/contact/*
Phone: (312) 629-6101
Email: admiss@saic.edu

COST OF ATTENDANCE:

Tuition & Fees: $53,360 | **Additional Expenses:** $21,200
Total: $74,560

Financial Aid: https://www.saic.edu/financial-aid/

ADDITIONAL INFORMATION:

Available Degree(s)

- BFA Studio, area: Painting and Drawing

Portfolio Requirement

Portfolios are required for incoming students. Submit 10-15 recent works.

Scholarships Offered

SAIC offers Presidential, Distinguished, Honors, Recognition, Incentive, and Enrichment scholarships at varied amounts. These merit scholarships are based on the student's portfolio and application materials. In addition, students who participated in certain art exhibitions or competitions may be eligible for the Competitive Excellence Award ($2000).

Need-based scholarships are also available. Some of these include the John and Mary E. Hoggins Scholarship for female SAIC students, the Roger Brown and George Veronda Scholarship, or the LeRoy Neiman Scholarship. Award amounts vary.

Special Opportunities

Studies at SAIC are interdisciplinary, where students do not declare a major and instead freely study among various areas of study. Students at SAIC have access to the internationally-recognized collection of the Art Institute of Chicago. This collection contains a body of work spanning 5,000 years from global artists. Students also have access to large, well-lit classrooms and studios to engage in open discussions and dialogue with faculty and classmates.

Notable Alumni

Samantha Bittman, Anko Chang, Jaye TC Cho, Laura Collins, Alice Cook, Jessica DuPreez, Colin Fleck, Weiyang Gao, Mary Griffin, Patrick Dean Hubbell, Tony Lewis, Kelly Lloyd, Kristy Luck, Ajmal 'Mas Man' Millar, Claire Moore, Aliza Nisenbaum, Ingrid Olson, Angel Otero, Zak Prekop, Celeste Rapone, Alejandro Rojas, Bassim Al Shaker, Margaux Siegel, Jeni Spota, Matthew Sprung, Adrienne Tarver, Alice Tippit, Orkideh Torabi, Maxwell Volkman, and Molly Zuckerman-Hartung

UNIVERSITY OF ILLINOIS, CHICAGO

Address: 1200 W Harrison St, Chicago, IL 60607
Website: *https://artandarthistory.uic.edu/bfa-studio-art*
Contact: *https://admissions.uic.edu/contact-admissions*
Phone: (312) 996-4350
Email: https://admissions.uic.edu/undergraduate/contact-undergraduate-admissions

COST OF ATTENDANCE:

In-State Tuition & Fees: $14,180 | **Additional Expenses:** $16,400
Total: $30,580

Out-of-State Tuition & Fees: $26,502 | **Additional Expenses:** $16,400
Total: $42,902

Financial Aid: https://financialaid.uic.edu/

ADDITIONAL INFORMATION:

Additional Degree(s)

- BFA Art, concentration: Studio Arts

Portfolio Requirement

There is no portfolio requirement for incoming students. However, students must undergo a portfolio review at the end of their first year to continue with the program.

Scholarships Offered

All incoming students are automatically considered for institutional scholarships. Students are encouraged to explore external scholarship opportunities. Most of the listed, institutional scholarship/grant opportunities at UIC are for Illinois residents. Residents may be eligible for the renewable Aim High Scholarship, a merit-based program that awards students up to $10,000 in tuition and fees. In addition, IL residents may be eligible for the Provost's Fellows Program, a merit-based scholarship that covers up to $5,000 of tuition and fees.

Special Opportunities

The BFA in Art program prepares students for contemporary art practice or advanced graduate study. Students who choose the Studio Arts concentration may further concentrate in either painting or sculpture. Intensive studio time enhances students' technical skills while seminars on art history and theory engage students to be critical thinkers. By senior year, students must produce a final BFA thesis exhibition.

Notable Alumni

Mark Aguhar, Angelina Gualdoni, Christopher Sperandio, and Alexa Viscius

ILLINOIS

INDIANA

IOWA

KANSAS

MICHIGAN

MINNESOTA

MISSOURI

NEBRASKA

NORTH DAKOTA

OHIO

SOUTH DAKOTA

WISCONSIN

MIDWEST

ILLINOIS

INDIANA

IOWA

KANSAS

MICHIGAN

MINNESOTA

MISSOURI

NEBRASKA

NORTH DAKOTA

OHIO

SOUTH DAKOTA

WISCONSIN

UNIVERSITY OF ILLINOIS URBANA-CHAMPAIGN (UIUC)

Address: 901 West Illinois Street, Urbana, IL 61801
Website: *https://art.illinois.edu/programs-and-applying/bachelors-programs/studio-art-ba-bfa/painting/*
Contact: *https://admissions.illinois.edu/contact*
Phone: (217) 333-0302
Email: admissions@illinois.edu

COST OF ATTENDANCE:

In-State Tuition & Fees: $16,866 | **Additional Expenses:** $16,194
Total: $33,060

Out-of-State Tuition & Fees: $34,316 | **Additional Expenses:** $16,534
Total: $50,850

Financial Aid: https://admissions.illinois.edu/Invest/financial-aid

ADDITIONAL INFORMATION:

Available Degree(s)

- BFA Studio Art, concentration: Painting
- BA Studio Art, concentration: Painting

Portfolio Requirement

Portfolios are required for incoming students. Submit 10 recent works.

Scholarships Offered

Both in-state and out-of-state applicants are eligible for various merit-based and need-based scholarships.

Special Opportunities

At UIUC, students undergo rigorous training in traditional drawing and painting techniques while also engaging in thoughtful dialogue about the cultural impact and complexities of the field. In the upper division coursework students may choose to focus on painting solely or explore drawing as well in forms such as graphic novels, character development, or community art.

Notable Alumni

Mark Staff Brandl, Christopher Brown, Annie Crawley, Greg Drasler, Leslie Erganian, Hart D. Fisher, Tom Goldenberg, David Klamen, Susan Rankaitis, Angela M. Rivers, Leo Segedin, Deb Sokolow, Lorado Taft, Charles H. Traub, Vivian Zapata, and Barbara Zeigler

DRAKE UNIVERSITY

Address: 2507 University Avenue, Des Moines, IA 50311
Website: *https://www.drake.edu/art-design/majorsminors/studioart/*
Contact: *https://www.drake.edu/admission/contact/*
Phone: (515) 271-3181
Email: https://www.drake.edu/admission/contact/

COST OF ATTENDANCE:

Tuition & Fees: $45,913 | **Additional Expenses:** $11,288
Total: $57,201

Financial Aid: https://www.financialaid.iastate.edu/

ADDITIONAL INFORMATION:

Available Degree(s)

- BFA Studio Art, concentrations: Drawing or Painting

Portfolio Requirement

There is no portfolio requirement for incoming students. There may be a portfolio review at some point during the student's undergraduate studies.

Scholarships Offered

Drake University offers numerous merit-based and need-based scholarships. Presidential Scholarships range from $22,000-$26,000 per year. Applicants are automatically considered for these awards and they are renewable as long as the student remains in good standing. Fine Arts Scholarships are available to select students who demonstrate exceptional talent.

Special Opportunities

In the Drawing concentration, students are given in-depth training to develop their technical skills. They are introduced to a variety of media and subject matter and are taught how to express their ideas effectively. Students in the Painting concentration develop competency with traditional materials and build their critical thinking skills. Students are challenged to utilize non-traditional materials and contemporary ideas to communicate visually.

Notable Alumni

Joanne Aono and Gwen M. Davidson

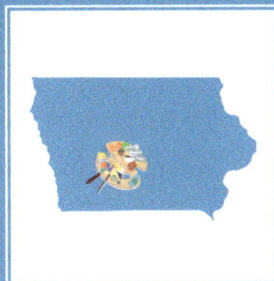

ILLINOIS

INDIANA

IOWA

KANSAS

MICHIGAN

MINNESOTA

MISSOURI

NEBRASKA

NORTH DAKOTA

OHIO

SOUTH DAKOTA

WISCONSIN

MIDWEST

ILLINOIS

INDIANA

IOWA

KANSAS

MICHIGAN

MINNESOTA

MISSOURI

NEBRASKA

NORTH DAKOTA

OHIO

SOUTH DAKOTA

WISCONSIN

MINNEAPOLIS COLLEGE OF ART & DESIGN

Address: 2501 Stevens Avenue, Minneapolis, MN 55404
Website: *https://www.mcad.edu/academics/undergraduate/majors/drawing-and-painting*
Contact: *https://mcad.edu/contact*
Phone: (612) 874-3700
Email: info@mcad.edu

COST OF ATTENDANCE:

Tuition & Fees: $49,452 | **Additional Expenses:** $7,640
Total: $57,092

Financial Aid: https://mcad.edu/admissions-and-aid/undergraduate/financial-aid

ADDITIONAL INFORMATION:

Available Degree(s)

- BFA Painting and Drawing
- BFA Fine Arts Studio

Portfolio Requirement

Portfolios are required for incoming students. Submit 8-16 works in any medium. Include the following four subjects: Landscape, Still Life, Interior Space, and Self-Portrait. At least one of these must be a drawing from direct observation. Include a full scale value. Submit via SlideRoom.

Scholarships Offered

MCAD Admissions Merit Scholarships are available to all incoming students. In addition, the MCAD Annual Merit Scholarship is a competition for students currently enrolled full-time and who have a 3.0+ GPA. Furthermore, students may earn scholarships through national competitions such as ARTS and the Scholastic Art Awards that MCAD will match. These matching scholarships are need-based.

Special Opportunities

Students in the Painting and Drawing program learn advanced techniques in 2D media while also engaging with guest artists through workshops. Students have 24/7 access to their individual studio spaces. The Fine Arts Studio program emphasizes critiques, pushing traditional boundaries of disciplines, and exploring the artist's role in society. Students who are more interested in the language of art rather than a specific type of medium may be better suited to this major.

Notable Alumni

Belle Baranceanu, Arnold Franz Brasz, Margaret Gove Camfferman, Theodore Haupt, Vance A. Larson, Jin Meyerson, George Morrison, Lisa Nankivil, Patricia Olson, and Clara Elsene Peck

UNIVERSITY OF MINNESOTA

Address: 330 21st Ave S., Minneapolis, MN 55455
Website: *https://cla.umn.edu/art/undergraduate/majors-minor/bfa-art*
Contact: *http://umn.force.com/admissions/*
Phone: (612) 625-6699
Email: admissions@umn.edu

COST OF ATTENDANCE:

In-State Tuition & Fees: $15,236 | **Additional Expenses:** $16,082
Total: $31,318

Out-of-State Tuition & Fees: $33,534 | **Additional Expenses:** $17,582
Total: $51,116

Financial Aid: https://admissions.tc.umn.edu/costsaid/index.html

ADDITIONAL INFORMATION:

Available Degree(s)

- BFA Art, concentration: Drawing, Painting, and Printmaking

Portfolio Requirement

There is no portfolio requirement for incoming students. Applicants may declare the BA in Art when they apply and then later apply for entry into the BFA program as an undergraduate. As an undergraduate, the student then must pass a portfolio review to gain entry to the BFA program.

Scholarships Offered

University of Minnesota offers numerous scholarship opportunities to all students, including in-state and out-of-state students. The University-Wide Academic Scholarships are highly competitive and have varying award amounts. In addition, all international students are automatically considered for the Global Excellence Scholarship ($10,000-$25,000 per year for up to four years).

Special Opportunities

The BFA Art program at University of Minnesota is highly selective and intensive. The Drawing, Painting, and Printmaking area of study explores traditional techniques and new forms. Students are encouraged to investigate the field of visual art while building their own personal approach. Interdisciplinary approaches are emphasized and critical thinking is practiced within the discipline.

Notable Alumni

Jim Denomie, Ivan Dmitri, Carol Hoorn Fraser, Harmony Hammond, Walter Kuhlman, Ralph Lemon, Terrance Lindall, Marjorie Mikasen, Michelle Muldrow, Doug Ohlson, Michael P. Price, Gordon Purcell, James Rosenquist, Deborah Rubin, Megan Rye, John Salminen, Maria Cristina Tavera, and Peter Verdoorn

ILLINOIS

INDIANA

IOWA

KANSAS

MICHIGAN

MINNESOTA

MISSOURI

NEBRASKA

NORTH DAKOTA

OHIO

SOUTH DAKOTA

WISCONSIN

MIDWEST

ILLINOIS

INDIANA

IOWA

KANSAS

MICHIGAN

MINNESOTA

MISSOURI

NEBRASKA

NORTH DAKOTA

OHIO

SOUTH DAKOTA

WISCONSIN

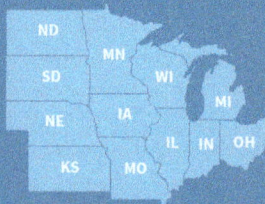

COLLEGE OF THE OZARKS

Address: 100 Opportunity Ave, Point Lookout, MO 65726
Website: *https://www.cofo.edu/Art#majors*
Contact: *https://www.cofo.edu/contact*
Phone: (800) 222-0525
Email: https://www.cofo.edu/Contact/Email

COST OF ATTENDANCE:

Tuition & Fees: $19,660 | **Additional Expenses:** $11,104
Total: $30,764

Financial Aid: https://www.cofo.edu/Scholarships

ADDITIONAL INFORMATION:

Available Degree(s)

- BA Art, emphasis: Studio Art

Portfolio Requirement

There is no portfolio requirement for incoming students.

Scholarships Offered

Room and Board scholarships are available through the Summer Work Education Program. The General Scholarship Application is also available to all students and closes December 1st each year. Furthermore, College of the Ozarks offers alumni and external scholarships.

Special Opportunities

College of the Ozarks houses the Boger Gallery, which frequently provides exhibitions for visiting artists. They also host many guest artists who lead workshops and lectures. Students in the Art program engage in critical thinking and develop their unique style.

Notable Alumni

Rose O'Neill

KANSAS CITY ART INSTITUTE

Address: 4415 Warwick Blvd., Kansas City, MO 64111
Website: *https://kcai.edu/academics/majors/painting/*
Contact: *https://kcai.edu/contact-us/*
Phone: (800) 522-5224
Email: admiss@kcai.edu

COST OF ATTENDANCE:

Tuition & Fees: $41,174 | **Additional Expenses:** $17,210
Total: $58,384

Financial Aid: https://kcai.edu/financial-aid-scholarships/

ADDITIONAL INFORMATION:

Available Degree(s)

- BFA Painting

Portfolio Requirement

Portfolios are required for incoming students. Submit at least 10 recent works. Submit via the student portal.

Scholarships Offered

KCAI merit scholarships are awarded to students annually as long as they maintain a cumulative GPA of 2.5+. In addition, the state of Missouri offers financial assistance grants to MO residents, such as Access Missouri and Bright Flight.

Special opportunities

Critical discourse is emphasized at KCAI. Students are encouraged to push beyond their comfort zones and experiment with various media. Traditional techniques and methods are taught, while new techniques are introduced. Double majors in Art History and Painting or Creative Writing and Painting are available.

Notable Alumni

Eric Bransby, Mary Ann Bransby, Dan Christensen, John Steuart Curry, Angela Dufresne, Amelia Ishmael, Paul Jenkins, Christian Holstad, Peregrine Honig, Suzanne Klotz, Barry Kooser, Arthur Kraft, Ronnie Landfield, Doris Lee, Ke-Sook Lee, Duard Marshall, Christina McPhee, Roger Medearis, Jackson Lee Nesbitt, Margot Peet, Robert Rauschenberg, Eric Sall, Nelson Shanks, Marjorie Strider, and Robert Templeton

ILLINOIS

INDIANA

IOWA

KANSAS

MICHIGAN

MINNESOTA

MISSOURI

NEBRASKA

NORTH DAKOTA

OHIO

SOUTH DAKOTA

WISCONSIN

MIDWEST

ILLINOIS

INDIANA

IOWA

KANSAS

MICHIGAN

MINNESOTA

MISSOURI

NEBRASKA

NORTH DAKOTA

OHIO

SOUTH DAKOTA

WISCONSIN

WASHINGTON UNIVERSITY IN ST. LOUIS

Address: 1 Brookings Dr., St. Louis, MO 63130
Website: *https://samfoxschool.wustl.edu/academics/college-of-art/bfa-ba-in-studio-art-and-design/studio-art*
Contact: *https://admissions.wustl.edu/contact-us/*
Phone: (314) 935-5858
Email: admissions@wustl.edu

COST OF ATTENDANCE:

Tuition & Fees: $57,750 | **Additional Expenses:** $19,016
Total: $76,766

Financial Aid: https://financialaid.wustl.edu/

ADDITIONAL INFORMATION:

Available Degree(s)

- BFA Studio Art, area: Painting

Portfolio Requirement

Portfolios are required for incoming students. Submit 10-20 works via SlideRoom.

Scholarships Offered

WashU offers merit-based and need-based scholarships for students in any major. Some of these institutional scholarships cover the full cost of tuition. They also offer the Signature Scholar Program, which involves individual applications and a weekend program. Partial and full tuition are offered within this scholarship program.

Special Opportunities

In the senior year, students must take a capstone course and deliver a public presentation about their work. BFA Studio Art majors participate in the Thesis Exhibition at the Des Lee Gallery in downtown St. Louis. Popular minors for Studio Art majors are Creative Practice for Social Change, Design, and Human-Computer Interaction.

Notable Alumni

Laylah Ali, Yu Araki, Patricia Degener, George Pearse Ennis, Bernard Fuchs, Cheryl Goldsleger, Veronica Helfensteller, Michael Joo, Kimia Ferdowski Kline, Ebony Patterson, Judy Pfaff, Dan Piraro, Jack Radley, Peter Saul, and Emmy Thelander

CLEVELAND INSTITUTE OF ART

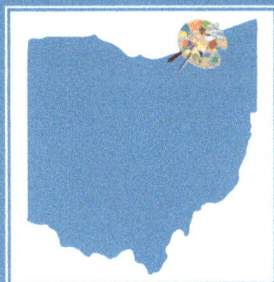

Address: 11610 Euclid Avenue, Cleveland, OH 44106
Website: *https://www.cia.edu/academics/drawing*
Contact: *https://www.cia.edu/contact*
Phone: (216) 421-7000
Email: admissions@cia.edu

COST OF ATTENDANCE:

Tuition & Fees: $45,495 | **Additional Expenses:** $17,010
Total: $62,505

Financial Aid: https://www.cia.edu/admissions/financing-your-education

ADDITIONAL INFORMATION:

Available Degree(s)

- BFA Drawing
- BFA Painting

Portfolio Requirement

Portfolios are required for incoming students. Submit 12-20 works via SlideRoom. Sketchbook pages are highly encouraged. Do not include works copied from photographs.

Scholarships Offered

CIA offers renewable merit scholarships to undergraduate students. Students are automatically considered upon acceptance. Students who do not receive a merit scholarship may still be considered for a need-based CIA grant if they submit a FAFSA.

Special Opportunities

CIA's Engage Practice is a feature of the school that provides students with the opportunity to work on real-world projects with external clients while they complete their studies. Students gain professional experience that will help them tremendously post-graduation. Drawing and Painting students learn to put their studio knowledge to work in a professional setting and are guided by faculty through this process.

Notable Alumni

Richard Anuszkiewicz, Samuel Bookatz, Leigh Brooklyn, Martha Elizabeth Burchfield Richter, Ray Burggraf, Rosana Castrillo Diaz, Shan Goshorn, Sante Graziani, Leamon Green, Mark Greenwold, Marsden Hartley, Bob Paul Kane, Victor Kord, Betty LaDuke, Robert Munford, Gertrude L. Pew, Glenora Richards, Jason Schoener, Jenny Scobel, Brain Shure, Judy Takács, Ann Toebbe, Frank N. Wilcox, Thaddeus Wolfe, and Harold Zisla

ILLINOIS

INDIANA

IOWA

KANSAS

MICHIGAN

MINNESOTA

MISSOURI

NEBRASKA

NORTH DAKOTA

OHIO

SOUTH DAKOTA

WISCONSIN

MIDWEST

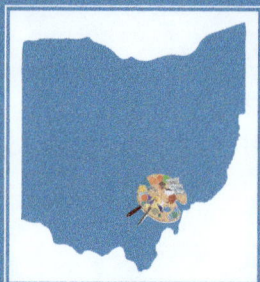

ILLINOIS

INDIANA

IOWA

KANSAS

MICHIGAN

MINNESOTA

MISSOURI

NEBRASKA

NORTH DAKOTA

OHIO

SOUTH DAKOTA

WISCONSIN

OHIO UNIVERSITY

Address: Ohio University, Athens, OH 45701
Website: *https://www.ohio.edu/fine-arts/art/undergraduate/bfa-studio-art/painting-drawing*
Contact: *https://www.ohio.edu/admissions/*
Phone: (740) 593-4818
Email: admissions@ohio.edu

COST OF ATTENDANCE:

In-State Tuition & Fees: $12,840 | **Additional Expenses:** $11,862
Total: $24,702

Out-of-State Tuition & Fees: $22,810 | **Additional Expenses:** $11,862
Total: $34,672

Financial Aid: https://www.ohio.edu/admissions/tuition/scholarships-financial-aid

ADDITIONAL INFORMATION:

Available Degree(s)

- BFA Studio Art, concentration: Painting + Drawing

Portfolio Requirement

Portfolios are required for incoming students. Submit 10 works.

Scholarships Offered

Students who submit their application by the Early Action deadline are automatically considered for the OHIO Excellence Awards. Award amounts vary. There is no separate application required.

Special Opportunities

Ohio University hosts visiting artists, guest lecturers, field trips, exhibitions, collaborative projects, and community engagement opportunities for BFA students. Students take foundational coursework in art history and studio techniques. Rigorous critiques, technical demonstrations, and an exploration into contemporary issues within the field are all a part of the program.

Notable Alumni

Alison Aune, Beth Campbell, Jim Dine, Jenny Holzer, Ronald Jones, Gloria Plevin, Roger Welch, and Maya Lin

ALABAMA

ARKANSAS

DELAWARE

DISTRICT OF
COLUMBIA

FLORIDA

GEORGIA

KENTUCKY

LOUISIANA

MARYLAND

MISSISSIPPI

NORTH CAROLINA

OKLAHOMA

SOUTH CAROLINA

TENNESSEE

TEXAS

VIRGINIA

WEST VIRGINIA

CHAPTER 13

REGION THREE

SOUTH

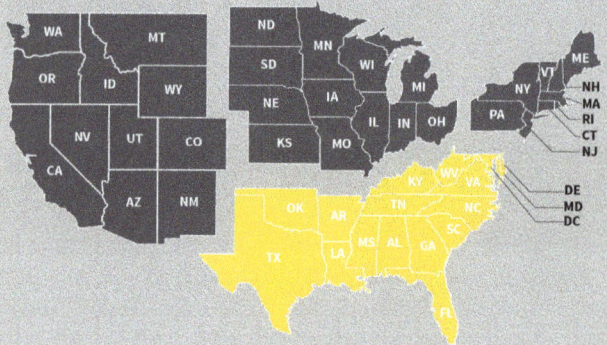

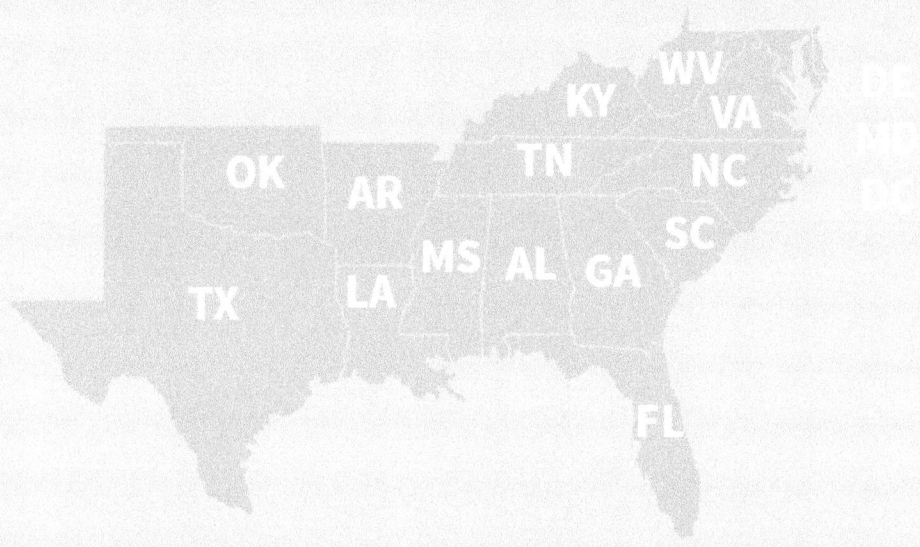

11 Programs 16 States

1. AR - Harding University
2. FL - Ringling College of Art and Design
3. FL – University of Miami
4. GA - Savannah College of Art and Design (SCAD)
5. MD - Maryland Institute College of Art
6. NC - University of North Carolina at Chapel Hill
7. TX - Texas Christian University
8. TX - The University of Houston
9. TX - The University of Texas at Austin
10. TX - The University of Texas at Dallas
11. VA - Virginia Commonwealth University

DRAWING & PAINTING PROGRAMS

School	Avg. GPA, SAT Evidence-Based Reading Writing (ERW), SAT Math (M), and ACT Composite (C) Early Decision (ED): Yes/No	Admission Statistics	Program(s)	Portfolio Required (req.)
Harding University 915 E. Market Ave., Searcy, AR 72149	GPA: N/A SAT (ERW): 540-650 SAT (M): 520-640 ACT (C): 21-29 ED: No	Overall College Admit Rate: 55% Undergrad Enrollment: 3,572 Total Enrollment: 4,617	BFA Visual Art Studio	Portfolio not req.
Ringling College of Art & Design 2700 N. Tamiami Trail, Sarasota, FL 34234	GPA: N/A SAT (ERW): N/A* SAT (M): N/A* ACT (C): N/A* *Test-optional ED: No	Overall College Admit Rate: 69% Undergrad Enrollment: 1,624 Total Enrollment: 1,624	BFA Fine Arts	Portfolio req.
University of Miami University of Miami, Coral Gables, FL 33124	GPA: 3.6 SAT (ERW): 620-700 SAT (M): 630-720 ACT (C): 28-32 ED: Yes	Overall College Admit Rate: 33% Undergrad Enrollment: 11,334 Total Enrollment: 17,809	BFA Studio Art, concentration: Painting	Portfolio not req.
Savannah College of Art & Design (SCAD) 342 Bull St., Savannah, GA 31401	GPA: 3.6 SAT (ERW): 540-640 SAT (M): 500-600 ACT (C): 20-27 ED: No	Admit Rate: 78% Undergrad Enrollment: 11,679 Total Enrollment: 14,265	BFA Painting	Portfolio req.

DRAWING & PAINTING PROGRAMS

School	Avg. GPA, SAT Evidence-Based Reading Writing (ERW), SAT Math (M), and ACT Composite (C) Early Decision (ED): Yes/No	Admission Statistics	Program(s)	Portfolio Required (req.)
Maryland Institute College of Art (MICA) 1300 W. Mount Royal Ave., Baltimore, MD 21217	GPA: N/A SAT (ERW): N/A SAT (M): N/A ACT (C): N/A *Test-optional ED: Yes	Admit Rate: 90% Undergrad Enrollment: 1,331 Total Enrollment: 1,892	BFA Drawing BFA Painting	Portfolio req.
University of North Carolina at Chapel Hill (UNC Chapel Hill) University of North Carolina, Chapel Hill, NC 27599	GPA: 4.39 SAT (ERW): 640-730 SAT (M): 640-760 ACT (C): 28-33 ED: No	Overall College Admit Rate: 25% Undergrad Enrollment: 19,395 Total Enrollment: 30,092	BA Studio Art BFA Studio Art	Portfolio not req.
Texas Christian University (TCU) 2800 South University Dr., Fort Worth, TX 76109	GPA: N/A SAT (ERW): 560-660 SAT (M): 550-660 ACT (C): 25-31 ED: No	Overall College Admit Rate: 48% Undergrad Enrollment: 9,704 Total Enrollment: 11,379	BA Studio Art BFA Studio Art, concentration: Painting	Portfolio req.
The University of Houston 4200 Elgin Street, Room 122, Houston, TX 77204	GPA: 3.73 SAT (ERW): 560-650 SAT (M): 560-660 ACT (C): 22-28 ED: No	Overall College Admit Rate: 63% Undergrad Enrollment: 39,165 Total Enrollment: 47,090	BFA Art, concentration: Painting	Portfolio req.

SOUTH

DRAWING & PAINTING PROGRAMS

School	Avg. GPA, SAT Evidence-Based Reading Writing (ERW), SAT Math (M), and ACT Composite (C) Early Decision (ED): Yes/No	Admission Statistics	Program(s)	Portfolio Required (req.)
The University of Texas at Austin (UT Austin) 310 Inner Campus Drive, Austin, TX 78712	GPA: N/A SAT (ERW): 610-720 SAT (M): 600-750 ACT (C): 26-33 ED: No	Overall College Admit Rate: 32% Undergrad Enrollment: 40,048 Total Enrollment: 50,476	BFA Studio Art, concentration: Painting & Drawing BA Studio Art	Portfolio req.
The University of Texas at Dallas (UT Dallas) 800 West Campbell Rd., Richardson, TX 75080	GPA: N/A SAT (ERW): 600-710 SAT (M): 620-740 ACT (C): 26-33 ED: No	Overall College Admit Rate: 79% Undergrad Enrollment: 21,187 Total Enrollment: 28,669	BA Visual and Performing Arts, concentration: Visual Arts	Portfolio not req.
Virginia Commonwealth University Virginia Commonwealth University, Richmond, VA 23284	GPA: 3.72 SAT (ERW): 540-640 SAT (M): 520-610 ACT (C): 21-28 ED: No	Admit Rate: 91% Undergrad Enrollment: 21,943 Total Enrollment: 29,070	BFA Painting and Printmaking	Portfolio req.

HARDING UNIVERSITY

Address: 915 E. Market Ave., Searcy, AR 72149
Website: *https://www.harding.edu/academics/colleges-departments/arts-humanities/art-design/fine-art*
Contact: *https://www.harding.edu/admissions/contact*
Phone: (800) 477-4407
Email: admissions@harding.edu

COST OF ATTENDANCE:

Tuition & Fees: $23,148 | **Additional Expenses:** $12,716
Total: $35,864

Financial Aid: https://www.harding.edu/finaid

ADDITIONAL INFORMATION:

Available Degree(s)

- BFA Visual Art Studio

Portfolio Requirement

There is no portfolio requirement for incoming students. However, a sophomore portfolio review is required after successful completion of the first undergraduate year.

Scholarships Offered

Harding University offers numerous merit and need-based scholarships that are renewable for four years as long as the student is in good academic standing. Awards include the Academic Achievement Scholarship, the Trustee Scholar Award, tuitioin discounts, and more. The Department of Art & Design offer scholarships to art students ranging from $600-$1,000 per year. A portfolio is required for this scholarship consideration.

Special Opportunities

The fine arts program at Harding University emphasizes molding the student into a professional artist or designer. Students learn technical skills, color theory, visual aesthestics, art history, and more. Electives include printmaking, ceramics, photography, watercolor, and computer graphics.

Notable Alumni

Tim Cox

RINGLING COLLEGE OF ART & DESIGN

Address: 2700 N. Tamiami Trail, Sarasota, FL 34234
Website: *https://www.ringling.edu/fine-arts/*
Contact: *https://www.ringling.edu/contact*
Phone: (941) 351–5100
Email: admissions@ringling.edu

COST OF ATTENDANCE:

Tuition & Fees: $49,649 | **Additional Expenses:** $22,025
Total: $71,674

Financial Aid: https://www.ringling.edu/financialaid

ADDITIONAL INFORMATION:

Available Degree(s)

- BFA Fine Arts

Portfolio Requirement

Portfolios are required for incoming students. Submit via SlideRoom. Applicants must include drawings from observation. Copying other artists is not permitted. Applicants must also avoid cliches, such as anime, tattoos, dragons, or unicorns.

Scholarships Offered

Ringling College offers merit scholarships and need-based grants. Some of the scholarships include the Presidential Scholarship ($25,000 per year for 4 years), the Dean's Scholarship ($10,000 per year for 4 years), the Faculty Scholarship ($8,000 per year for 4 years) and several others.

Special Opportunities

Students in the Fine Arts program build upon their critical thinking, painting, drawing, sculpture, printmaking, and technology skills. They are given designated studio spaces and have access to facilities and exhibition opportunities in Ringling's Studios North facility. This area is exclusive to Fine Arts students.

Notable Alumni

Melvin Gomez, Kevin Llewellyn, Tim Jaeger, Andrew Jones, Tim Rogerson, Stephen Scott Young, and Mike Zeck

ALABAMA

ARKANSAS

DELAWARE

DISTRICT OF COLUMBIA

FLORIDA

GEORGIA

KENTUCKY

LOUISIANA

MARYLAND

MISSISSIPPI

NORTH CAROLINA

OKLAHOMA

SOUTH CAROLINA

TENNESSEE

TEXAS

VIRGINIA

WEST VIRGINIA

SOUTH

ALABAMA

ARKANSAS

DELAWARE

DISTRICT OF
COLUMBIA

FLORIDA

GEORGIA

KENTUCKY

LOUISIANA

MARYLAND

MISSISSIPPI

NORTH CAROLINA

OKLAHOMA

SOUTH CAROLINA

TENNESSEE

TEXAS

VIRGINIA

WEST VIRGINIA

UNIVERSITY OF MIAMI

Address: 1223 Dickinson Drive, Coral Gables, FL 33146
Website: *https://art.as.miami.edu/programs/undergraduate-programs/painting--drawing/index.html*
Contact: *https://admissions.miami.edu/undergraduate/about/contact-us/index.html*
Phone: (305) 284 3731
Email: admission@miami.edu

COST OF ATTENDANCE:

Tuition & Fees: $53,682 | **Additional Expenses:** $20,030
Total: $73,712

Financial Aid: https://finaid.miami.edu/index.html

ADDITIONAL INFORMATION:

Available Degree(s)

- BFA Studio Art, concentration: Painting

Portfolio Requirement

There is no portfolio requirement for incoming students. However, students must undergo a portfolio review during their undergraduate studies.

Scholarships Offered

The most prestigious merit award at UM is the Stamps Scholarship. This scholarship covers the student's full cost of attendance for four years of study, including a laptop allowance and access to a $12,000 enrichment fund that may be used towards educational purposes. Other UM scholarships also cover the full cost of tuition or cost of attendance for all four years. These are all based on merit and/or financial need.

Special Opportunities

University of Miami emphasizes building rendering skills and technical abilities and then applying these skills to original art. The university houses facilities available to all art students, such as the printmaking studio, foundational drawing classes, a computer lab, exhibition spaces, and studio spaces for ceramics, glass, sculpture, painting, photography, and digital media students.

Notable Alumni

Xavier Cortada, Joel Resnicof, and Grace Slick

SAVANNAH COLLEGE OF ART & DESIGN (SCAD)

Address: 342 Bull St., Savannah, GA 31401
Website: *https://www.scad.edu/academics/programs/painting*
Contact: *https://www.scad.edu/about/contact*
Phone: (912) 525-5100
Email: contact@scad.edu
Other locations: Atlanta, GA

COST OF ATTENDANCE:

Tuition & Fees: $38,340 | **Additional Expenses:** $15,269
Total: $53,609

Financial Aid: https://www.scad.edu/admission/financial-aid-and-scholarships

ADDITIONAL INFORMATION:

Available Degree(s)

- BFA Painting

Portfolio Requirement

Portfolios are required for incoming students. Applicants may choose any of the following categories, whether or not it reflects their intended major: Business & Marketing, Visual Art, Time-Based Media, Writing, Equestrian, or Performing Arts. However, SCAD suggests applicants should curate a portfolio that demonstrates the applicant's interests and aptitude. Submit via SlideRoom.

Scholarships Offered

All applicants including international students are eligible for merit-scholarships. The May and Paul Poetter Scholarship awards full tuition and is based on academic achievement. The Frances Larkin McCommon Scholarship awards full tuition and is based on artistic achievement. SCAD also offers SCAD academic scholarships ($1,500-$12,000). Among grants, the SCAD Athletic Grant awards $2,000-$12,000. Furthermore, students may receive a scholarship award via the SCAD Challenge Scholarship. Awards range from $2,000-$4,000.

Special Opportunities

At SCAD, students engage in technical skill-building while also networking with students and alumni. SCAD's painting students have access to the SCAD Museum of Art and may attend classes, film screenings, gallery talks, annual events, lectures, workshops, and more. Minors that complement the program include photography, printmaking, sculpture, and art history.

Notable Alumni

Luna Brothers, M. Alice LeGrow, and Meredith Pardue

ALABAMA

ARKANSAS

DELAWARE

DISTRICT OF COLUMBIA

FLORIDA

GEORGIA

KENTUCKY

LOUISIANA

MARYLAND

MISSISSIPPI

NORTH CAROLINA

OKLAHOMA

SOUTH CAROLINA

TENNESSEE

TEXAS

VIRGINIA

WEST VIRGINIA

SOUTH

MARYLAND INSTITUTE COLLEGE OF ART (MICA)

Address: 1300 W. Mount Royal Ave., Baltimore, MD 21217
Website: *https://www.mica.edu/undergraduate-majors-minors/drawing-major/*
Contact: *https://www.mica.edu/mica-dna/contact-us/*
Phone: (410) 669-9200
Email: https://www.mica.edu/forms/contact-undergraduate-admission/

COST OF ATTENDANCE:

Tuition & Fees: $53,333 | **Additional Expenses:** $17,820
Total: $71,153

Financial Aid: https://www.mica.edu/financial-aid/

ADDITIONAL INFORMATION:

Available Degree(s)

- BFA Drawing
- BFA Painting

Portfolio Requirement

Portfolios are required for incoming students. Submit 12-20 works. MICA strongly suggests including drawings from observation rather than from imagination or copied from photographs.

Scholarships Offered

MICA offers several, competitive merit-based scholarships to all incoming undergraduate students. Some of these offers include the Mathias J. Devito Scholarship Program ($40,000 over 4 years), the Fanny B. Thalheimer Scholarship ($16,000-$68,000 over four years), the Academic Excellence Scholarships ($12,000-$24,000) and several others.

Special Opportunities

Drawing and Painting majors have independent studio spaces, housed at MICA's Fred Lazarus IV Studio Center. This historical building is a short walk from the main campus. MICA's students in the two programs have interned at the studios of artists such as Tony Shore and Sherry Wolf.

Notable Alumni

Dhruvi Acharya, Kamrooz Aram, Donald Baechler, Angie Elizabeth Brooksby, Larry Poncho Brown, Jeremy Caniglia, Lesley Dill, William Downs, Danielle Eckhardt, John Ennis, Brock Enright, Joan Erbe, Amir H. Fallah, Joshua Field, Lee Gatch, GLadys Goldstein, Elaine Hamilton, Douglas Hoffman, Earl Hoffman, Kika Karadi, Morris Louis, Ted Mineo, Karin Olah, Selma L. Oppenheimer, Amalie Rothschild, Shelby Shackelford, Amy Sherald, and Lee Woodward Zeigler

ALABAMA
ARKANSAS
DELAWARE
DISTRICT OF COLUMBIA
FLORIDA
GEORGIA
KENTUCKY
LOUISIANA
MARYLAND
MISSISSIPPI
NORTH CAROLINA
OKLAHOMA
SOUTH CAROLINA
TENNESSEE
TEXAS
VIRGINIA
WEST VIRGINIA

UNIVERSITY OF NORTH CAROLINA AT CHAPEL HILL

Address: University of North Carolina, Chapel Hill, NC 27599
Website: *https://art.unc.edu/courses-and-degrees/studio-art-undergraduate-programs/undergraduate-program-in-studio-art/*
Contact: *https://www.unc.edu/about/contact-us/*
Phone: (919) 962-2211
Email: https://www.unc.edu/about/contact-us/

COST OF ATTENDANCE:

In-State Tuition & Fees: $9,018 | **Additional Expenses:** $15,248
Total: $24,266

Out-of-State Tuition & Fees: $36,000 | **Additional Expenses:** $16,026
Total: $52,026

Financial Aid: https://studentaid.unc.edu/

ADDITIONAL INFORMATION:

Available Degree(s)

- BA Studio Art
- BFA Studio Art

Portfolio Requirement

There is no portfolio requirement for incoming students. However, students may be required to undergo a portfolio review for the BFA during their undergraduate studies.

Scholarships Offered

UNC at Chapel Hill offers many need-based and merit-based scholarship opportunities for students. Most are for students who are residents of North Carolina. Students may consider applying for external opportunities as well. Some require students to apply by the early action deadline.

Special Opportunities

At UNC, students are highly encouraged to take part in study abroad and extend their intellectual horizons. The Department of Art suggests students to explore fellowship opportunities such as the Frances L. Phillips Travel Scholarship, the Dwayne Lowder Study Abroad Art Scholarships, and more. UNC also has study abroad affiliate programs with the Glasgow School of Art in Scotland and the Lorenzo de Medici Institute in Florence, Italy.

Notable Alumni

Howard Little and Ben Long

ALABAMA
ARKANSAS
DELAWARE
DISTRICT OF COLUMBIA
FLORIDA
GEORGIA
KENTUCKY
LOUISIANA
MARYLAND
MISSISSIPPI
NORTH CAROLINA
OKLAHOMA
SOUTH CAROLINA
TENNESSEE
TEXAS
VIRGINIA
WEST VIRGINIA

SOUTH

ALABAMA

ARKANSAS

DELAWARE

DISTRICT OF
COLUMBIA

FLORIDA

GEORGIA

KENTUCKY

LOUISIANA

MARYLAND

MISSISSIPPI

NORTH CAROLINA

OKLAHOMA

SOUTH CAROLINA

TENNESSEE

TEXAS

VIRGINIA

WEST VIRGINIA

TEXAS CHRISTIAN UNIVERSITY (TCU)

Address: 2800 South University Dr., Fort Worth, TX 76109
Website: *https://finearts.tcu.edu/art/academics/areas-of-study/studio-art/*
Contact: *https://admissions.tcu.edu/connect.php*
Phone: (817) 257-7000
Email: frogmail@tcu.edu

COST OF ATTENDANCE:

Tuition & Fees: $51,660 | **Additional Expenses:** $20,168
Total: $71,828

Financial Aid: https://financialaid.tcu.edu/

ADDITIONAL INFORMATION:

Available Degree(s)

- BA Studio Art
- BFA Studio Art, concentration: Painting

Portfolio Requirement

Portfolios are required for incoming students. Submit 15-20 works. Applicants are instructed to include drawings from life and to avoid adding any works copied from photographs.

Scholarships Offered

The Nordan Fine Arts Awards are competitive scholarships for students in the College of Fine Arts. The Nordan Young Artist Award is $10,000+ for incoming freshmen, based on application audition. Students may then renew this scholarship for their remaining years.

Special Opportunities

At TCU, Studio Art majors frequently participate in exhibition opportunities and internship opportunities for artists or volunteer work as gallery attendants. Coursework offered in the program includes painting, printmaking, drawing, sculpture, ceramics, photography, life studies, video art, art history, and more.

Notable Alumni

Glenda Green and Mary McCleary

THE UNIVERSITY OF HOUSTON

Address: 4200 Elgin Street, Room 122, Houston, TX 77204
Website: *https://uh.edu/kgmca/art/undergraduate-programs/painting/*
Contact: *https://www.uh.edu/undergraduate-admissions/discover/* meet-your-counselor/
Phone: (713) 743-2400
Email: admissions@uh.edu

COST OF ATTENDANCE:

In-State Tuition & Fees: $11,569 | **Additional Expenses:** $11,110
Total: $22,679

Out-of-State Tuition & Fees: $26,839 | **Additional Expenses:** $11,110
Total: $37,949

Financial Aid: https://uh.edu/undergraduate-admissions/cost/index.php

ADDITIONAL INFORMATION:

Available Degree(s)

- BFA Art, concentration: Painting

Portfolio Requirement

Portfolios are required for incoming students. Submit a 250-word statement and 2-4 works created within the past two years.

Scholarships Offered

University scholarships based on merit and/or demonstrated need are available to all students. For instance, the Academic Excellence scholarship gifts an award of up to $6,000 per year.

Special Opportunities

At UH, painting students are encouraged to experiment with mediums, utilize critical thinking skills, and become proficient with using the tools and materials necessary to visually communicate their ideas. Internships are available for students at commercial galleries such as the DiverWorks Artspace, Lawndale Art Center, the Museum of Fine Arts, Houston, and The Contemporary Arts Museum. Students may also become gallery assistants, exhibitaion preparators, curatorial and research assistants, or education and outreach program assistants.

Notable Alumni

Michael Ray Charles, Cheryl Kelley, and Julian Schnabel

ALABAMA

ARKANSAS

DELAWARE

DISTRICT OF COLUMBIA

FLORIDA

GEORGIA

KENTUCKY

LOUISIANA

MARYLAND

MISSISSIPPI

NORTH CAROLINA

OKLAHOMA

SOUTH CAROLINA

TENNESSEE

TEXAS

VIRGINIA

WEST VIRGINIA

SOUTH

THE UNIVERSITY OF TEXAS AT AUSTIN (UT AUSTIN)

Address: 310 Inner Campus Drive, Austin, TX 78712
Website: *https://art.utexas.edu/undergraduate/majors/studio-art*
Contact: *https://admissions.utexas.edu/contact*
Phone: (512) 471-1922
Email: admissions@austin.utexas.edu

COST OF ATTENDANCE:

In-State Tuition & Fees: $10,824 | **Additional Expenses:** $16,904
Total: $27,728

Out-of-State Tuition & Fees: $38,326 | **Additional Expenses:** $16,904
Total: $55,230

Financial Aid: https://finaid.utexas.edu/

ADDITIONAL INFORMATION:

Available Degree(s)

- BFA Studio Art, concentration: Painting & Drawing
- BA Studio Art

Portfolio Requirement

Portfolios are required for incoming students for both the BFA and BA programs. Submit 12 works and an artist statement. At least 2 of your works must be from direct observation.

Scholarships Offered

UT Austin offers many scholarships to incoming students. Students are encouraged to apply by December 1st to be automatically considered. Applicants are also encouraged to submit a FAFSA or the Texas Application for State Financial Aid (TASFA) by January 15th for need-based aid. Students may still be considered for merit scholarships even if they do not submit a FAFSA.

Special opportunities

At UT Austin, the five areas of study are crafted in the BFA program are in pairs to expand the mediums students work with. Students may choose to study Painting & Drawing, Photography & Media, Transmedia, or Print, Sculpture, & Expanded Media. UT Austin hosts visiting artists in workshops and lectures that seniors may help organize.

Notable Alumni

Mark Aguhar, Natalia Anciso, and Thomas Darnell

ALABAMA

ARKANSAS

DELAWARE

DISTRICT OF COLUMBIA

FLORIDA

GEORGIA

KENTUCKY

LOUISIANA

MARYLAND

MISSISSIPPI

NORTH CAROLINA

OKLAHOMA

SOUTH CAROLINA

TENNESSEE

TEXAS

VIRGINIA

WEST VIRGINIA

THE UNIVERSITY OF TEXAS AT DALLAS (UT DALLAS)

Address: 800 West Campbell Rd., Richardson, TX 75080
Website: *https://www.utdallas.edu/fact-sheets/ah/ba-visual-and-performing-arts/*
Contact: *https://enroll.utdallas.edu/contact/*
Phone: (972) 883-2111
Email: admission@utdallas.edu

COST OF ATTENDANCE:

In-State Tuition & Fees: $16,412 | **Additional Expenses:** $17,132
Total: $33,544

Out-of-State Tuition & Fees: $44,812 | **Additional Expenses:** $17,132
Total: $61,944

Financial Aid: https://www.utdallas.edu/finaid/

ADDITIONAL INFORMATION:

Available Degree(s)

- BA Visual and Performing Arts, concentration: Visual Arts

Portfolio Requirement

There is no portfolio requirement for incoming students.

Scholarships Offered

UT Dallas offers various merit-based and need-based awards to all students. The Eugene McDermott Award is a generous scholarship program that offers full tuition, a living stipend, $1000 yearly book stipend, $12,000 fund for study abroad, travel expenses for cohort trips, tickets to various cultural events, $3,000 fund for personal development, and travel home twice yearly. UT Dallas also offers the Academic Excellence Scholarship Awards, which provides varied awards towards tuition and fees. Several other institutional scholarships are available.

Special Opportunities

At UT Dallas, Visual and Performing Arts (VPA) students manage long-term projects, learn critical and analytical thinking skills, contribute to meaningful discourse, and engage in studio work. Students may earn honors by completing an honors thesis/project if they wish to. ADditionally, exceptional undergraduates who meet certain academic requirements may be considered for the Fast Track admission to graduate school. This allows students to work on their master's degree before graduating with their bachelor's.

Notable Alumni

Brian Fridge

ALABAMA

ARKANSAS

DELAWARE

DISTRICT OF COLUMBIA

FLORIDA

GEORGIA

KENTUCKY

LOUISIANA

MARYLAND

MISSISSIPPI

NORTH CAROLINA

OKLAHOMA

SOUTH CAROLINA

TENNESSEE

TEXAS

VIRGINIA

WEST VIRGINIA

SOUTH

ALABAMA

ARKANSAS

DELAWARE

DISTRICT OF
COLUMBIA

FLORIDA

GEORGIA

KENTUCKY

LOUISIANA

MARYLAND

MISSISSIPPI

NORTH CAROLINA

OKLAHOMA

SOUTH CAROLINA

TENNESSEE

TEXAS

VIRGINIA

WEST VIRGINIA

VIRGINIA COMMONWEALTH UNIVERSITY

Address: Virginia Commonwealth University, Richmond, VA 23284
Website: *https://arts.vcu.edu/academics/departments/painting-printmaking/*
Contact: *https://www.vcu.edu/contacts/*
Phone: (804) 828-0100
Email: ugrad@vcu.edu

COST OF ATTENDANCE:

In-State Tuition & Fees: $17,140 | **Additional Expenses:** $17,549
Total: $34,689

Out-of-State Tuition & Fees: $38,478 | **Additional Expenses:** $17,549
Total: $56,027

Financial Aid: https://finaid.vcu.edu/

ADDITIONAL INFORMATION:

Available Degree(s)

- BFA Painting and Printmaking

Portfolio Requirement

Portfolios are required for incoming students. Submit 12-16 works created over the past two years. Applicants are encouraged to include drawings from observation and discouraged to include copied work.

Scholarships Offered

First-year students may be eligible for VCUarts talent scholarships ($5,000-$12,000 annually) if they apply by January 15th. Students are automatically considered and eligibility is based on academic merit and artistic talent. In addition, all students are automatically considered for institutional scholarships if they apply by November 15th. University scholarship awards vary based on the scholarship, but range from $8,000 per year to $16,000 plus room and board per year.

Special Opportunities

Students at VCU frequently travel and learn more about artistic influence in various communities. Visits to galleries, museums, and studios across the country and the world are encouraged. Students in the Painting and Printmaking program build technical skills and participate in socially-engaged practices, creative coding, video, perforamnce, and more. All students are also encouraged to participate in the annual program to Peru each summer.

Notable Alumni

Trudy Benson, James Bumgardner, Rose Datoc Dall, Torkwase Dyson, Sterling Hundley, Abby Kasonik, and Carol Sutton

CHAPTER 14

REGION FOUR

WEST

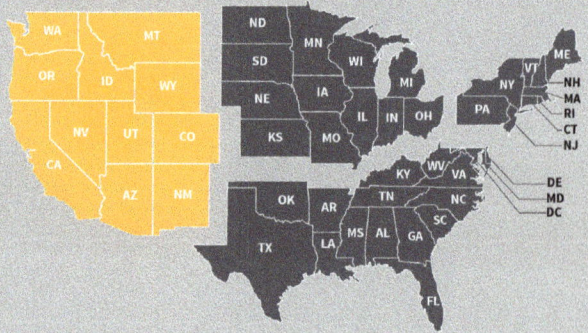

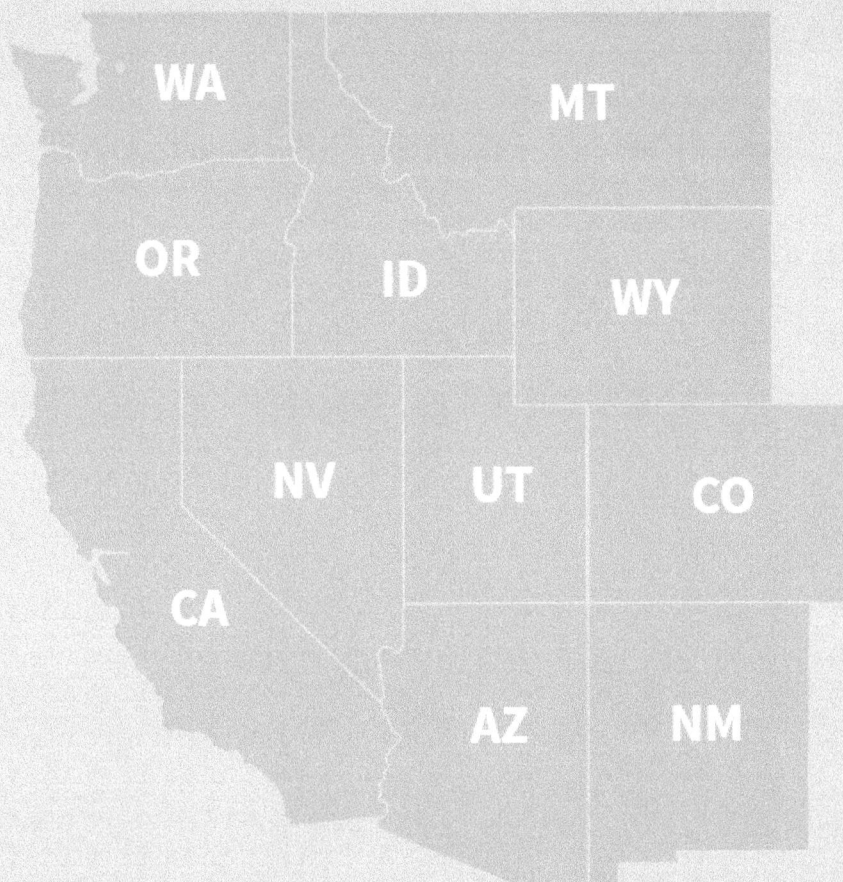

10 Programs | 13 States

1. *AZ – Arizona State University*
2. *CA - ArtCenter College of Design*
3. *CA - California College of the Arts*
4. *CA - California Institute of the Arts*
5. *CA - Laguna College of Art and Design*
6. *CA - University of California, Irvine*
7. *CA - University of California, Los Angeles*
8. *OR - University of Oregon*
9. *WA - University of Puget Sound*
10. *WA - University of Washington*

DRAWING & PAINTING PROGRAMS

School	Avg. GPA, SAT Evidence-Based Reading Writing (ERW), SAT Math (M), and ACT Composite (C) Early Decision (ED): Yes/No	Admission Statistics	Program(s)	Portfolio Required (req.)
Arizona State University 1151 S. Forest Ave. Tempe, AZ 85281	GPA: N/A SAT (ERW): 550-650 SAT (M): 550-670 ACT (C): 21-28 *Test-optional ED: No	Admit Rate: 88% Undergrad Enrollment: 63,124 Total Enrollment: 74,795	BFA Art, concentration: Drawing BFA Art, concentration: Painting BFA Art, concentration: Drawing & Painting	Portfolio not req.
ArtCenter College of Design 1700 Lida St, Pasadena, CA 91103	GPA: N/A SAT (ERW): N/A* SAT (M): N/A* ACT (C): N/A* *Test-optional ED: No	Overall College Admit Rate: 76% Undergrad Enrollment: 1,912 Total Enrollment: 2,182	BFA Fine Art, concentration: Fine Art BFA Fine Art, concentration: Painting and Illustration	Portfolio req.
California College of the Arts (CCA) 1111 Eighth St., San Francisco, CA 94107	GPA: N/A SAT (ERW): N/A* SAT (M): N/A* ACT (C): N/A* *Test-optional]ED: No	Overall College Admit Rate: 85% Undergrad Enrollment: 1,239 Total Enrollment: 1,612	BFA Painting & Drawing	Portfolio req.
California Institute of the Arts (CalArts) 24700 McBean Pkwy., Valencia, CA 91355	GPA: N/A SAT (ERW): N/A* SAT (M): N/A* ACT (C): N/A* *Test-optional]ED: Yes	Overall College Admit Rate: 32% Undergrad Enrollment: 783 Total Enrollment: 1,189	BFA Art	Portfolio req.

School	Avg. GPA, SAT Evidence-Based Reading Writing (ERW), SAT Math (M), and ACT Composite (C) Early Decision (ED): Yes/No	Admission Statistics	Program(s)	Portfolio Required (req.)
Laguna College of Art and Design 2222 Laguna Canyon Rd., Laguna Beach, CA 92651	GPA: N/A SAT (ERW): 710-760 SAT (M): 770-800 ACT (C): 34-36]ED: No	Admit Rate: 83% Undergrad Enrollment: 732 Total Enrollment: 782	BFA Drawing + Painting	Portfolio req.
University of California, Irvine (UCI) 4000 Mesa Rd., Irvine, CA 92697	GPA: N/A SAT (ERW): 600-680 SAT (M): 630-750 ACT (C): 26-33]ED: No	Overall College Admit Rate: 30% Undergrad Enrollment: 29,638 Total Enrollment: 36,303	BA Art, emphasis: Painting & Drawing	Portfolio not req.
University of California, Los Angeles (UCLA) 405 Hilgard Avenue, Los Angeles, CA 90095	GPA: 3.9 SAT (ERW): 650-740 SAT (M): 640-780 ACT (C): 29-34]ED: No	Overall College Admit Rate: 14% Undergrad Enrollment: 31,636 Total Enrollment: 44,589	BA Art, area: Painting & Drawing	Portfolio req.
University of Oregon 5249 University of Oregon, Eugene, OR 97403	GPA: 3.65 SAT (ERW): 550-650 SAT (M): 540-640 ACT (C): 22-29]ED: No	Overall College Admit Rate: 84% Undergrad Enrollment: 18,045 Total Enrollment: 21,752	BFA Art, concentration: Painting and Drawing]BA Art, concentration: Painting and Drawing	Portfolio not req.

WEST

DRAWING & PAINTING PROGRAMS

School	Avg. GPA, SAT Evidence-Based Reading Writing (ERW), SAT Math (M), and ACT Composite (C) Early Decision (ED): Yes/No	Admission Statistics	Program(s)	Portfolio Required (req.)
University of Puget Sound 1500 N. Warner Street, Tacoma, WA 98416	GPA: N/A SAT (ERW): N/A* SAT (M): N/A* ACT (C): N/A* *Test-optional]ED: Yes	Overall College Admit Rate: 87% Undergrad Enrollment: 1,898 Total Enrollment: 2,130	BA Studio Art, specialization: Painting	Portfolio not req.
University of Washington 1400 NE Campus Parkway, Seattle, WA, 98195	GPA: 3.82 SAT (ERW): 590-700 SAT (M): 610-753 ACT (C): 27-33]ED: No	Overall College Admit Rate: 56% Undergrad Enrollment: 32,244 Total Enrollment: 48,149	BA Art, concentration: Painting + Drawing	Portfolio not req.

ARIZONA STATE UNIVERSITY

Address: 1151 S. Forest Ave. Tempe, AZ 85281
Website: *https://art.asu.edu/degree-programs/drawing-painting?dept=1622&id=1*
Contact: *https://admission.asu.edu/findmyrep*
Phone: (480) 965-7788
Email: admissions@asu.edu

COST OF ATTENDANCE:

In-State Tuition & Fees: $10,710 | **Additional Expenses:** $20,811
Total: $31,521

Out-of-State Tuition & Fees: $28,800 | **Additional Expenses:** $21,561
Total: $50,361

Financial Aid: https://students.asu.edu/financial-aid

ADDITIONAL INFORMATION:

Available Degree(s)

- BFA Art, concentration: Drawing
- BFA Art, concentration: Painting
- BFA Art, concentration: Drawing & Painting

Portfolio Requirement

Portfolios are not required for incoming students. However, a portfolio review may be required during BFA students' undergraduate studies.

Scholarships Offered

ASU offers many merit-based and need-based scholarships for all students. The New American University Scholars is for high achieving students. This award is for residents, nonresidents, transfer students, and international students.

Special Opportunities

Students in the Painting and/or Drawing concentrations utilize multiple studio spaces that contain media such as watercolor, oil paints, drawing media, and multimedia. Critiques, seminars, visiting artist presentations, and exhibitions are all held at the Martin Wong Studio on campus. Senior undergraduates are also eligible to have private studios.

Notable Alumni

Alvin Eli Amason, Jonni Cheatwood, Dan Lam, and Holly Roberts

ARTCENTER COLLEGE OF DESIGN

Address: 1700 Lida St, Pasadena, CA 91103
Website: *https://www.artcenter.edu/academics/undergraduate-degrees/fine-art/overview.html*
Contact: *http://www.artcenter.edu/admissions/contact.html*
Phone: (626) 396-2373
Email: admissions@artcenter.edu

COST OF ATTENDANCE:

Tuition & Fees: $49,653 | **Additional Expenses:** $24,820
Total: $74,473

Financial Aid: https://www.artcenter.edu/admissions/tuition-and-aid/tuition-and-fees/tuition.html

ADDITIONAL INFORMATION:

Available Degree(s)

- BFA Fine Art, concentration: Fine Art
- BFA Fine Art, concentration: Painting and Illustration

Portfolio Requirement

Portfolios are required for incoming students. Submit 15-20 works in any media that demonstrate an exploration of concepts and how you examine ideas visually. Applicants seeking to minor in Illustration should include 4-6 figure drawings from a live model.

Scholarships Offered

ArtCenter awards merit-based and need-based scholarships to students. Students with an exceptional portfolio are awarded up to $25,000.

Special Opportunities

Studio spaces at ArtCenter contain ample light and are held in a newly-renovated building that houses the Fine Art and Illustration departments. With 47 studio spaces, BFA students are encouraged to interact with one another and build a sense of community.

Notable Alumni

Doug Aitken, Lynn Aldrich, Edgar Arceneaux, Carol Bennett, Clayton Brothers, Lawrence Carroll, Tom Christopher, Lindsay Dawson, Eyvind Earle, James Gurney, Frank Hagel, Thomas KInkade, Melissa Kretschmer, Sharon Lockhart, Richard MacDonald, PAtrick Martinez, Rebeca Méndez, Craig Mullins, Bob Peak, Jorge Pardo, Mark Ryden, Sterling Ruby, Stan Sakai, Ken Shutt, Gordon Smedt, Jeff Soto, Jennifer Steinkamp, Mark Tansey, Diana Thater, Shirley Tse, Richard Wagener, Casey Weldon, Jack Wemp, Pae White, and Charles Wysocki

ALASKA

ARIZONA

CALIFORNIA

COLORADO

HAWAII

IDAHO

MONTANA

NEVADA

NEW MEXICO

OREGON

UTAH

WASHINGTON

WYOMING

WEST

ALASKA

ARIZONA

CALIFORNIA

COLORADO

HAWAII

IDAHO

MONTANA

NEVADA

NEW MEXICO

OREGON

UTAH

WASHINGTON

WYOMING

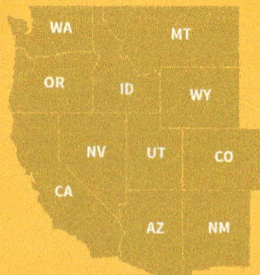

CALIFORNIA COLLEGE OF THE ARTS (CCA)

Address: 1111 Eighth St., San Francisco, CA 94107
Website: *https://www.cca.edu/fine-arts/painting-drawing/*
Contact: *Contact via phone or email.*
Phone: (800) 447-1278
Email: info@cca.edu

COST OF ATTENDANCE:

Tuition & Fees: $54,726 | **Additional Expenses:** $25,255
Total: $79,981

Financial Aid: https://www.cca.edu/admissions/tuition/#section-financial-aid

ADDITIONAL INFORMATION:

Available Degree(s)

- BFA Painting & Drawing

Portfolio Requirement

Portfolios are required for incoming students. Submit 10-15 works via SlideRoom.

Scholarships Offered

Merit-based, need-based, CCA-named, and other scholarships available.

Special Opportunities

Rigorous critique and interdisciplinary approaches are at the heart of teaching at CCA. Students build their technical and conceptual skills via intensive studio coursework and engage in dialogue with faculty, peers, and visiting artists. During the third year, students receive their own studio space and then upgrade to a larger space in their last year. This individualized space allows students to complete their thesis projects. Community projects and student-led events, such as the Figure Drawing Night, all build community within the program.

Notable Alumni

Natalia Anciso, Robert Bechtle, Clifford Beck, Henrietta Berk, Val Britton, David Bierk, Squeak Carnwath, Geoffrey Chadsey, Jules de Balincourt, George Albert Harris, Warren Leopold, Jake Longstreth, Louis Macouillard, Richard McLean, George Miyasaki, Robert S. Neuman, Toyin Odutola, Nathan Oliveira, Suzanna Scheuer, M. Louise Stanley, Don Stivers, James Torlakson, and Lee Weiss

CALIFORNIA INSTITUTE OF THE ARTS (CALARTS)

Address: 24700 McBean Pkwy., Valencia, CA 91355
Website: *https://art.calarts.edu/programs/art/bfa*
Contact: *https://calarts.edu/about/contact*
Phone: (661) 255-1050
Email: admissions@calarts.edu

COST OF ATTENDANCE:

Tuition & Fees: $53,466 | **Additional Expenses:** $20,792
Total: $74,258

Financial Aid: https://calarts.edu/tuition-and-financial-aid/
financial-aid/overview

ADDITIONAL INFORMATION:

Available Degree(s)

- BFA Art

Portfolio Requirement

Portfolios are required for incoming students. Submit 15-20 recent works via SlideRoom. Applicants are also strongly encouraged to submit a 30-90-second introduction video.

Scholarships Offered

CalArts offers institutional scholarships that are awarded to students based on need and merit. All awards cover tuition only. In addition, they offer endowed and annually funded scholarships.

Special Opportunities

At the start of the BFA Art program, students investigate art-historical traditions, theory, and various media. Coursework includes seminars, group critiques, and independent studies. By the third year, students pursue their independent studio projects. Most upper-level students also receive their own individual studio space.

Notable Alumni

Jeremy Blake, Nayland Blake, Ross Bleckner, Barbara Bloom, John S. Boskovich, Krista Buecking, JAmes CAsebere, Heather Cassils, Richard K. Diran, Sam Durant, Eric Fischl, Mike Kelley, Rodney McMillian, John Miller, Rubén Ortiz-Torres, Tony Oursler, Michael Polish, Gala Porras-Kim, Monique Prieto, and David Salle

ALASKA

ARIZONA

CALIFORNIA

COLORADO

HAWAII

IDAHO

MONTANA

NEVADA

NEW MEXICO

OREGON

UTAH

WASHINGTON

WYOMING

WEST

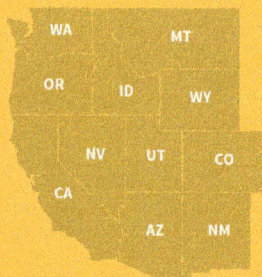

LAGUNA COLLEGE OF ART AND DESIGN

Address: 2222 Laguna Canyon Rd., Laguna Beach, CA 92651
Website: *https://www.lcad.edu/drawing-painting/program/program-overview*
Contact: *https://www.lcad.edu/contact*
Phone: (949) 376-6000
Email: admissions@lcad.edu

COST OF ATTENDANCE:

Tuition & Fees: $32,600 | **Additional Expenses:** $23,979
Total: $56,579

Financial Aid: https://www.lcad.edu/admissions/tuition-financial-aid/financial-aid

ADDITIONAL INFORMATION:

Available Degree(s)

- BFA Drawing + Painting

Portfolio Requirement

Portfolios are required for incoming students. Submit 12-20 recent works. LCAD suggests including observational works, life drawings, sketchbook pages that show process work, and master study works.

Scholarships Offered

The LCAD Institutional Grant is a merit-based scholarship that is based on academics and the admissions portfolio. This scholarship is renewable each year the student is at LCAD provided they remain in good academic standing. It is recommended that students apply for outside scholarships as well.

Special Opportunities

The BFA program at LCAD is grounded in classical traditions. Students are taught the necessary skills to accurately portray still life, figure, portrait, landscape, and group figures. They are also taught how to communicate visually through narrative storytelling. Furthermore, the business of art is also incorporated into the curriculum. Professional practices, marketing, and presentation are all skills that students have by the time they graduate.

Notable Alumni

Candice Bohannon, Stefan Cummings, Angela Cunningham, Matt Dickson, Alia El-Bermani, James Galindo, Frank Gonzalez, Miguel Gonzalez, Emily Gordon, Ja'Rie Gray, Michael Harnish, Adam Harrison, Jason Kowalski, Alex Krigbaum, Brianna Lee, Elizabeth McGhee, Andrew Myers, Charity Oetgen, Carolin Peters, Christopher Ramsey, Brittany Ryan, Fatima Silva, Adrienne Stein, Eric Stoner, and Jason Umfress

UNIVERSITY OF CALIFORNIA, IRVINE

Address: 4000 Mesa Rd., Irvine, CA 92697
Website: *https://art.arts.uci.edu/undergraduate-areas-emphasis*
Contact: *https://www.admissions.uci.edu/contact.php*
Phone: (949) 824-6614
Email: admissions@uci.edu

COST OF ATTENDANCE:

In-State Tuition & Fees: $15,621 | **Additional Expenses:** $20,420
Total: $36,041

Out-of-State Tuition & Fees: $45,375 | **Additional Expenses:** $20,420
Total: $65,795

Financial Aid: https://www.ofas.uci.edu/content/

ADDITIONAL INFORMATION:

Available Degree(s)

- BA Art, emphasis: Painting & Drawing

Portfolio Requirement

Portfolios are not required for incoming students.

Scholarships Offered

UCI offers numerous scholarships that are merit-based and/or need-based and are for residents, nonresidents, international students, or undocumented students. UCI's Distinguished Scholarships are merit-based and range from $3,000 per year to over $10,000. International and undocumented students with financial need are eligible for $3,000 through the Anteater Uplift Scholarship.

Special Opportunities

UCI houses two large studio spaces for painting and drawing students. Technical skills and analytical thinking are emphasized in this program. Students may also take coursework in other areas, such as Performance Art, Photography, Digital Filmmaking, Electronic Art and Design, Sculpture, or Critical Theory.

Notable Alumni

Michael Asher, Dan Bayles, Chris Burden, Erica Cho, Garnet Hertz, Tom Jancar, Barbara T. Smith, and James Turrell

ALASKA

ARIZONA

CALIFORNIA

COLORADO

HAWAII

IDAHO

MONTANA

NEVADA

NEW MEXICO

OREGON

UTAH

WASHINGTON

WYOMING

WEST

ALASKA

ARIZONA

CALIFORNIA

COLORADO

HAWAII

IDAHO

MONTANA

NEVADA

NEW MEXICO

OREGON

UTAH

WASHINGTON

WYOMING

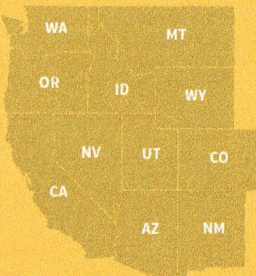

UNIVERSITY OF CALIFORNIA, LOS ANGELES

Address: 405 Hilgard Avenue, Los Angeles, CA 90095
Website: *https://www.art.ucla.edu/areas-of-study/painting-drawing/*
Contact: *https://admission.ucla.edu/contact*
Phone: (310) 206-8441
Email: https://admission.ucla.edu/contact/admission-representatives

COST OF ATTENDANCE:

In-State Tuition & Fees: $13,239 | **Additional Expenses:** $22,096
Total: $35,335

Out-of-State Tuition & Fees: $42,993 | **Additional Expenses:** $22,096
Total: $65,089

Financial Aid: https://www.financialaid.ucla.edu/

ADDITIONAL INFORMATION:

Available Degree(s)

- BA Art, area: Painting & Drawing

Portfolio Requirement

Portfolios are required for incoming students. Submit 8-10 works.

Scholarships Offered

Students may apply for scholarships through the MyUCLA portal. Additionally, UCLA offers the Regents Scholarship for students who demonstrate academic excellence. Up to 100 are awarded per year.

Special Opportunities

Experimentation with media and critical thinking are foundational tenets of the BA program at UCLA. Students are encouraged to broaden their perceptual awareness and discuss the historical and contemporary precedents for the work they produce. UCLA houses five spacious studio classrooms that overlook Los Angeles. Six individual senior studio spaces are awarded by a portfolio review. Students also may utilize the wood shop or printmaking studio.

Notable Alumni

Amy Adler, Sara Kathryn Arledge, Glenna Avila, GAry Baseman, Edith Baumann, Slater Bradley, Vija Celmins, Coleman Collins, Jennifer Dalton, Alyce Frank, Charles Garabedian, Gilah Yelin Hirsch, Jane Jin Kaisen, Craig Kauffman, Annie Lapin, Linda Levi, Edward Meshekoff, Meleko Mokgosi, Ed Moses, Alexandra Nechita, Tameka Norriss, Raymond Pettibon, Jason Rhoades, Betye Saar, Ben Sakoguchi, Shizu Saldamando, Sarah Seager, Cindy Shih, Jan Stussy, Wu Tsang, Idelle Weber, Jan Wurm, and Richard Wyatt Jr.

UNIVERSITY OF OREGON

Address: 5249 University of Oregon, Eugene, OR 97403
Website: *https://artdesign.uoregon.edu/art/undergrad/bfa/art-concentration*
Contact: *https://admissions.uoregon.edu/contact*
Phone: (541) 346-3656
Email: admissions@uoregon.edu

COST OF ATTENDANCE:

In-State Tuition & Fees: $15,054 | **Additional Expenses:** $14,640
Total: $29,694

Out-of-State Tuition & Fees: $41,700 | **Additional Expenses:** $14,640
Total: $56,340

Financial Aid: https://financialaid.uoregon.edu/

ADDITIONAL INFORMATION:

Available Degree(s)

- BFA Art, concentration: Painting and Drawing
- BA Art, concentration: Painting and Drawing

Portfolio Requirement

Portfolios are not required for incoming students. However, a portfolio review is required to move onto the BFA program after completing undergraduate art coursework at the University of Oregon.

Scholarships Offered

The Architects Foundation Diversity Scholarships, need-based aid, and university-wide scholarships offer varying award amounts and opportunities. University-wide scholarships include the Stamps Scholarship (four years of full tuition, fees, room & board, and up to $12,000 in enrichment funds), the Presidential Scholarship ($36,000 over four years), Diversity Excellence Scholarship ($6500), and more.

Special Opportunities

Students in the Painting and Drawing concentration of either the BA or BFA learn the basic techniques of drawing and oil painting as well as how to translate visual experience to one's work. Critical thinking skills are heavily emphasized in these programs. Students also learn how to sustain an artistic practice and they learn about the historical context and contemporary possibilities for the field.

Notable Alumni

Gordon GIlkey, LaVerne Krause, Suzie Liles, Susan Lowdermilk, Eric Norstad, Joe Sacco, Heidi Schwegler, Charles Stokes, Ron Wigginton, and Russel Wong

ALASKA

ARIZONA

CALIFORNIA

COLORADO

HAWAII

IDAHO

MONTANA

NEVADA

NEW MEXICO

OREGON

UTAH

WASHINGTON

WYOMING

WEST

ALASKA

ARIZONA

CALIFORNIA

COLORADO

HAWAII

IDAHO

MONTANA

NEVADA

NEW MEXICO

OREGON

UTAH

WASHINGTON

WYOMING

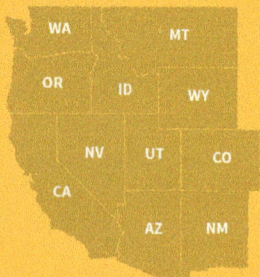

UNIVERSITY OF PUGET SOUND

Address: 1500 N. Warner Street, Tacoma, WA 98416
Website: *https://www.pugetsound.edu/academics/art-art-history*
Contact: *https://admit.washington.edu/contact/*
Phone: (206) 543-9686
Email: Contact via contact link.

COST OF ATTENDANCE:

In-State Tuition & Fees: $12,076 | **Additional Expenses:** $18,564
Total: $30,640

Out-of-State Tuition & Fees: $39,906 | **Additional Expenses:** $18,564
Total: $58,470

Financial Aid: https://www.washington.edu/financialaid/

ADDITIONAL INFORMATION:

Available Degree(s)

- BA Studio Art, specialization: Painting

Portfolio Requirement

Portfolios are not required for incoming students.

Scholarships Offered

All incoming students are automatically considered for merit aid worth up to $30,000. These include the Founders, Alumni, Faculty, Dean's, President's, Trustee, and Provost Scholarships. Awards are renewable for up to ten semesters.

Special Opportunities

Art students at the University of Puget Sound may take coursework in a variety of areas. Elective coursework examples include Beginning Printmaking, The Art of Mexico & Mesoamerica, East Asian Calligraphy, and more. Painting students have studio spaces with skylights and their own storage and workstation areas. Students also have access to the ceramics building and the printmaking studio.

Notable Alumni

Dale Chihuly

UNIVERSITY OF WASHINGTON

Address: University of Washington, Seattle, WA 98195
Website: *https://art.washington.edu/art/ba-art-painting-drawing-concentration*
Contact: *https://admit.washington.edu/contact/*
Phone: (206) 543-9686
Email: Contact via contact link.

COST OF ATTENDANCE:

In-State Tuition & Fees: $12,076 | **Additional Expenses:** $18,564
Total: $30,640

Out-of-State Tuition & Fees: $39,906 | **Additional Expenses:** $18,564
Total: $58,470

Financial Aid: https://www.washington.edu/financialaid/

ADDITIONAL INFORMATION:

Available Degree(s)

- BA Art, concentration: Painting + Drawing

Portfolio Requirement

Portfolios are not required for incoming students.

Scholarships Offered

UW offers several types of institutional aid for all students. Washington residents that show exceptional leadership and community engagement may be eligible for the Presidential Scholarship (valued at $10,000). All U.S. citizens may be eligible for the Purple & Gold Scholarship. High-need, high achieving students are eligible for the UW Diversity Scholarship ($10,000 per year for four years).

Special Opportunities

Students in the Painting & Drawing concentration start by solidifying a strong base in drawing before moving onto fundamental techniques for painting. Some of the coursework Art students take include Intro to Ceramics, Intro to Sculpture, Works on Paper, Narratives in Art & Design, Color Studies, Intro to Glass, and more. An art history class is also required, and student smay choose from a variety of courses, such as: Athena to Lady Gaga: Art in the Modern Imagination, Chinese Art & Visual Culture, Art of India: Mohenjo-Daro to the Mughals, Paris Architecture, and more.

Notable Alumni

Deborah Aschheim, Bennett Bean, Nancy Carman, F. Lennox Campello, Dan Corson, Fredericka Foster, and Norie Sato

ALASKA
ARIZONA
CALIFORNIA
COLORADO
HAWAII
IDAHO
MONTANA
NEVADA
NEW MEXICO
OREGON
UTAH
WASHINGTON
WYOMING

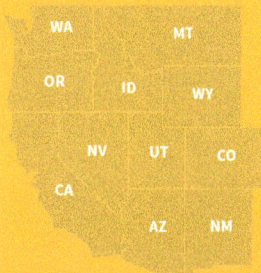

WEST

CHAPTER 15

DRAWING AND PAINTING SCHOOLS ALPHABETIZED BY CITY/STATE

School	City	State
Arizona State University	Tempe	Arizona
Harding University	Searcy	Arkansas
University of California, Irvine (UCI)	Irvine	California
Laguna College of Art and Design	Laguna Beach	California
University of California, Los Angeles (UCLA)	Los Angeles	California
ArtCenter College of Design	Pasadena	California
California College of the Arts	San Francisco	California
California Institute of the Arts	Valencia	California
Yale University	New Haven	Connecticut
University of Miami	Coral Gables	Florida
Ringling College of Art and Design	Sarasota	Florida
Savannah College of Art and Design	Savannah	Georgia
University of Illinois Urbana-Champaign (UIUC)	Champaign	Illinois
American Academy of Art College	Chicago	Illinois
School of the Art Institute Chicago	Chicago	Illinois
University of Illinois, Chicago	Chicago	Illinois
Bradley University	Peoria	Illinois
Drake University	Des Moines	Iowa
Maryland Institute College of Art	Baltimore	Maryland
Boston University	Boston	Massachusetts
Massachusetts College of Art & Design	Boston	Massachusetts
Minneapolis College of Art & Design	Minneapolis	Minnesota
University of Minnesota, Twin Cities	Minneapolis	Minnesota
Kansas City Art Institute	Kansas City	Missouri
College of the Ozarks	Point Lookout	Missouri
Washington University, St. Louis	St. Louis	Missouri
Rutgers, The State University of New Jersey	New Brunswick	New Jersey
Bard College	Annandale-On-Hudson	New York
Pratt Institute	Brooklyn	New York
SUNY Buffalo	Buffalo	New York
Columbia University	New York	New York
Cooper Union	New York	New York
CUNY Hunter College	New York	New York
Parsons School of Design	New York	New York
School of Visual Arts	New York	New York
Syracuse University	Syracuse	New York

School	City	State
University of North Carolina at Chapel Hill	Chapel Hill	North Carolina
Ohio University	Athens	Ohio
Cleveland Institute of Art	Cleveland	Ohio
University of Oregon	Eugene	Oregon
Arcadia University	Glenside	Pennsylvania
Pennsylvania Academy of Fine Arts (PAFA) + University of Pennsylvania	Philadelphia	Pennsylvania
Temple University	Philadelphia	Pennsylvania
Providence College	Providence	Rhode Island
Rhode Island School of Design	Providence	Rhode Island
The University of Texas at Austin (UT Austin)	Austin	Texas
Texas Christian University	Fort Worth	Texas
The University of Houston	Houston	Texas
The University of Texas at Dallas (UT Dallas)	Richardson	Texas
Virginia Commonwealth University	Richmond	Virginia
University of Washington	Seattle	Washington
University of Puget Sound	Tacoma	Washington

CHAPTER 16

DRAWING AND PAINTING SCHOOLS BY AVERAGE TEST SCORE

DRAWING AND PAINTING SCHOOLS BY AVERAGE GPA

School	Avg. GPA
College of the Ozarks	3.37
Temple University	3.48
Ohio University	3.55
Savannah College of Art and Design	3.6
University of Miami	3.6
University of Oregon	3.65
Syracuse University	3.67
Arcadia University	3.7
Drake University	3.7
SUNY Buffalo	3.7
Virginia Commonwealth University	3.72
The University of Houston	3.73
Cooper Union	3.75
Boston University	3.76
Pratt Institute	3.82
University of Washington	3.82
Bradley University	3.83
University of California, Los Angeles (UCLA)	3.9
Washington University, St. Louis	4.21
University of North Carolina at Chapel Hill	4.39
University of Minnesota, Twin Cities	3.53
American Academy of Art College	N/A
Arizona State University	N/A
ArtCenter College of Design	N/A
Bard College	N/A
California College of the Arts	N/A
California Institute of the Arts	N/A
Cleveland Institute of Art	N/A
Columbia University	N/A
CUNY Hunter College	N/A
Harding University	N/A
Kansas City Art Institute	N/A
Laguna College of Art and Design	N/A
Maryland Institute College of Art	N/A
Massachusetts College of Art & Design	N/A
Minneapolis College of Art & Design	N/A

School	Avg. GPA
Parsons School of Design	N/A
Pennsylvania Academy of Fine Arts (PAFA) + University of Pennsylvania	N/A
Providence College	N/A
Rhode Island School of Design	N/A
Ringling College of Art and Design	N/A
Rutgers, The State University of New Jersey	N/A
School of the Art Institute Chicago	N/A
School of Visual Arts	N/A
Texas Christian University	N/A
The University of Texas at Austin (UT Austin)	N/A
The University of Texas at Dallas (UT Dallas)	N/A
University of California, Irvine (UCI)	N/A
University of Illinois Urbana-Champaign (UIUC)	N/A
University of Illinois, Chicago	N/A
University of Puget Sound	N/A
Yale University	N/A

DRAWING AND PAINTING SCHOOLS BY AVERAGE SAT SCORE

School	Avg. SAT
College of the Ozarks	470-540 (ERW) 480-560 (M)
University of Illinois, Chicago	510-610 (ERW) 520-640 (M)
Arcadia University	520-630 (ERW) 510-600 (M)
University of Minnesota, Twin Cities	530-620 (ERW) 520-640 (M) *Test-optional
Ohio University	530-630 (ERW) 520-620 (M)
Bradley University	540-630 (ERW) 540-650 (M)
Savannah College of Art and Design	540-640 (ERW) 500-600 (M)
Virginia Commonwealth University	540-640 (ERW) 520-610 (M)
Harding University	540-650 (ERW) 520-640 (M)
School of Visual Arts	545-650 (ERW) 530-680 (M)
University of Oregon	550-650 (ERW) 540-640 (M)
Arizona State University	550-650 (ERW) 550-670 (M) *Test-optional
SUNY Buffalo	560-640 (ERW) 580-670 (M)
The University of Houston	560-650 (ERW) 560-660 (M)
School of the Art Institute Chicago	560-660 (ERW) 480-600 (M)

School	Avg. SAT
Texas Christian University	560-660 (ERW) 550-660 (M)
Drake University	560-660 (ERW) 550-680 (M)
Cleveland Institute of Art	560-680 (ERW) 510-620 (M)
Pratt Institute	570-660 (ERW) 550-680 (M)
CUNY Hunter College	580-650 (ERW) 590-690 (M)
Parsons School of Design	580-680 (ERW) 560-680 (M)
Rutgers, The State University of New Jersey	580-680 (ERW) 600-730 (M)
University of Washington	590-700 (ERW) 610-753 (M)
University of Illinois Urbana-Champaign (UIUC)	590-700 (ERW) 620-770 (M)
University of California, Irvine (UCI)	600-680 (ERW) 630-750 (M)
The University of Texas at Dallas (UT Dallas)	600-710 (ERW) 620-740 (M)
Providence College	610-680 (ERW) 600-680 (M)
Rhode Island School of Design	610-700 (ERW) 640-770 (M)
The University of Texas at Austin (UT Austin)	610-720 (ERW) 600-750 (M)
University of Miami	620-700 (ERW) 630-720 (M)
Boston University	640-720 (ERW) 670-780 (M)
University of North Carolina at Chapel Hill	640-730 (ERW) 640-760 (M)
University of California, Los Angeles (UCLA)	640-740 (ERW) 640-790 (M)
Cooper Union	650-740 (ERW) 655-790 (M)
Washington University, St. Louis	720-760 (ERW) 760-800 (M)
Columbia University	720-770 (ERW) 740-800 (M)
Yale University	720-780 (ERW) 740-800 (M)
American Academy of Art College	N/A
Syracuse University	N/A
ArtCenter College of Design	N/A *Test optional
Bard College	N/A *Test optional
California College of the Arts	N/A *Test optional
California Institute of the Arts	N/A *Test optional
Kansas City Art Institute	N/A *Test optional
Laguna College of Art and Design	N/A *Test optional
Maryland Institute College of Art	N/A *Test optional
Massachusetts College of Art & Design	N/A *Test optional
Minneapolis College of Art & Design	N/A *Test optional
Pennsylvania Academy of Fine Arts (PAFA) + University of Pennsylvania	N/A *Test optional
Ringling College of Art and Design	N/A *Test optional
Temple University	N/A *Test optional
University of Puget Sound	N/A *Test optional

DRAWING AND PAINTING SCHOOLS BY AVERAGE ACT SCORE

School	Avg. ACT C
College of the Ozarks	18-23
Cleveland Institute of Art	19-27
Savannah College of Art and Design	20-27
Arcadia University	20-28
Ohio University	21-26
University of Minnesota, Twin Cities	21-26 *Test-optional
Virginia Commonwealth University	21-28
Arizona State University	21-28 *Test-optional
University of Illinois, Chicago	21-29
Harding University	21-29
School of the Art Institute Chicago	22-25
The University of Houston	22-28
Bradley University	22-28
University of Oregon	22-29
School of Visual Arts	23-27
SUNY Buffalo	23-29
Drake University	23-30
Pratt Institute	25-30
CUNY Hunter College	25-31
Texas Christian University	25-31
Rutgers, The State University of New Jersey	25-32
Parsons School of Design	26-30
The University of Texas at Austin (UT Austin)	26-33
The University of Texas at Dallas (UT Dallas)	26-33
University of California, Irvine (UCI)	26-33
Providence College	27-31
Rhode Island School of Design	27-32
University of Illinois Urbana-Champaign (UIUC)	27-33
University of Washington	27-33
University of California, Los Angeles (UCLA)	27-34
University of Miami	28-32
University of North Carolina at Chapel Hill	28-33
Boston University	30-34
Cooper Union	30-35

School	Avg. ACT C
Yale University	33-35
Columbia University	33-35
Washington University, St. Louis	33-35
American Academy of Art College	N/A
Syracuse University	N/A
ArtCenter College of Design	N/A *Test optional
Bard College	N/A *Test optional
California College of the Arts	N/A *Test optional
California Institute of the Arts	N/A *Test optional
Kansas City Art Institute	N/A *Test optional
Laguna College of Art and Design	N/A *Test optional
Maryland Institute College of Art	N/A *Test optional
Massachusetts College of Art & Design	N/A *Test optional
Minneapolis College of Art & Design	N/A *Test optional
Pennsylvania Academy of Fine Arts (PAFA) + University of Pennsylvania	N/A *Test optional
Ringling College of Art and Design	N/A *Test optional
Temple University	N/A *Test optional
University of Puget Sound	N/A *Test optional

CHAPTER 17

TOP 15 SCHOOLS IN DRAWING AND PAINTING

S/N	School Name
1	Yale University
2	Rhode Island School of Design
3	School of the Art Institute of Chicago
4	Columbia University
5	Bard College
6	Boston University
7	Maryland Institute College of Art
8	University of California, Los Angeles
9	California Institute of the Arts
10	Hunter College (CUNY)
11	Pratt Institute
12	School of Visual Arts
13	Virginia Commonwealth University
14	Cranbrook Academy of Art
15	Temple University

JOURNEY TO ART, DANCE, MUSIC, THEATRE, FILM, AND FASHION SERIES

JOURNEY TO

Fashion Design

COLLEGE ADMISSIONS & PROFILES

RACHEL A. WINSTON, PH.D.

JOURNEY TO

Fashion Merchandising

COLLEGE ADMISSIONS & PROFILES

RACHEL A. WINSTON, PH.D.

JOURNEY TO

Costume Design & Technical Theatre

COLLEGE ADMISSIONS & PROFILES

RACHEL A. WINSTON, PH.D.

JOURNEY TO

Theatre and the Dramatic Arts

COLLEGE ADMISSIONS & PROFILES

RACHEL A. WINSTON, PH.D.

JOURNEY TO
Musical
Theatre
COLLEGE ADMISSIONS & PROFILES
RACHEL A. WINSTON, PH.D.

JOURNEY TO
Architecture
COLLEGE ADMISSIONS & PROFILES
RACHEL A. WINSTON, PH.D.

JOURNEY TO
Photography
COLLEGE ADMISSIONS & PROFILES
FASHION, SPORTS, ART, TRAVEL, & JOURNALSM
RACHEL A. WINSTON, PH.D.

JOURNEY TO
Illustration
and
Comic Book Design
COLLEGE ADMISSIONS & PROFILES
RACHEL A. WINSTON, PH.D.

JOURNEY TO
Drawing
and
Painting
COLLEGE ADMISSIONS & PROFILES

RACHEL A. WINSTON, PH.D.

JOURNEY TO
Industrial &
Product Design
COLLEGE ADMISSIONS & PROFILES

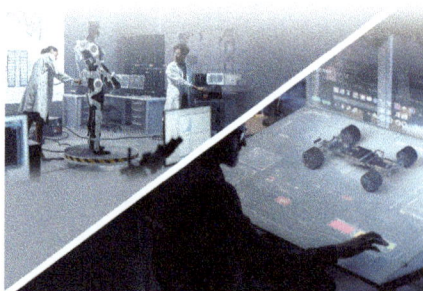

RACHEL A. WINSTON, PH.D.

JOURNEY TO
3-D
Art & Design
COLLEGE ADMISSIONS & PROFILES
SCULPTURE, CERAMICS,
GLASS, & JEWELRY DESIGN

RACHEL A. WINSTON, PH.D.

JOURNEY TO
Graphic Design,
Advertising,
& Public Relations
COLLEGE ADMISSIONS & PROFILES

RACHEL A. WINSTON, PH.D.

JOURNEY TO
Film Directing & Production

COLLEGE ADMISSIONS & PROFILES
FILM, TELEVISION, & MEDIA ARTS

RACHEL A. WINSTON, PH.D.

JOURNEY TO
Screenwriting & Film and Cinema Studies

COLLEGE ADMISSIONS & PROFILES
WRITING, CULTURE, HISTORY, & CRITICAL ANALYSIS

RACHEL A. WINSTON, PH.D.

Live your dreams today remembering that discipline is the bridge between dreams and achievement!

"We believe in the American Dream that all people rich or poor can go as far in life as their talents and persistence will take them."

– Lizard Publishing Vision

At Lizard, we help you make your dreams come true.

CONTACT INFORMATION

Phone: 949-833-7706

E-mail: collegeguide@yahoo.com

Website: collegelizard.com and Lizard-publishing.com

COMPREHENSIVE HEALTH CARE SERIES

DENTAL SCHOOL
PREPARATION, APPLICATION, ADMISSION

YOUR JOURNEY, YOUR FUTURE

**LEIGH MOORE, D.M.D.
AND RACHEL A. WINSTON, Ph.D.**

DENTAL SCHOOL PROFILES

*Dental School Admissions
Data and Analysis*

RACHEL A. WINSTON, PH.D.
Researcher, Professor, Admissions Expert, Motivational Speaker

MEDICAL SCHOOL
PREPARATION, APPLICATION, ADMISSION

YOUR JOURNEY, YOUR FUTURE

**RACHEL A. WINSTON, PH.D.
AND LEIGH MOORE, D.D.S.**

MEDICAL SCHOOL PROFILES

*Medical School Admissions
Data and Analysis*

RACHEL A. WINSTON, PH.D.
Researcher, Professor, Admissions Expert, Motivational Speaker

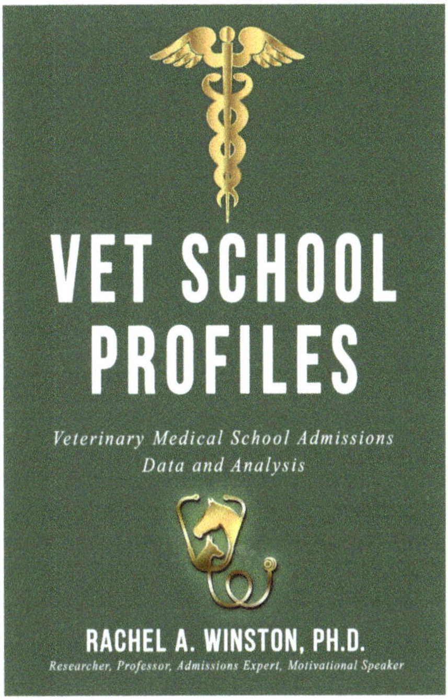

PHARM.D. SCHOOL
PREPARATION, APPLICATION, ADMISSION

YOUR JOURNEY, YOUR FUTURE

RACHEL A. WINSTON, PH.D.
Researcher, Professor, Admissions Expert, Motivational Speaker

PHARM.D. SCHOOL PROFILES

Pharmacy School Admissions Data and Analysis

RACHEL A. WINSTON, PH.D.
Researcher, Professor, Admissions Expert, Motivational Speaker

OSTEOPATHIC MEDICAL SCHOOL
PREPARATION, APPLICATION, ADMISSION

YOUR JOURNEY, YOUR FUTURE

RACHEL A. WINSTON, PH.D.
Researcher, Professor, Admissions Expert, Motivational Speaker

OSTEO SCHOOL PROFILES

Osteopathic Medical School Admissions Data and Analysis

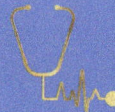

RACHEL A. WINSTON, PH.D.
Researcher, Professor, Admissions Expert, Motivational Speaker

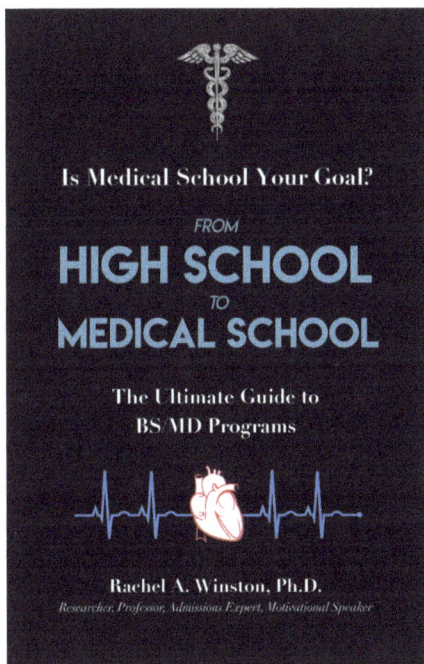

INDEX

Symbols

A

B

C

D

G

H

I

J

K

L

M

N

O

P

R

S

212

T

U

V

W

Y

Z